Attaining Leadership

Knowing and Leading Yourself, First!

Linda Dougherty

Leaders must know themselves first to lead themselves, and, then others. And, the challenge with leadership is that a leader must have the right culture plus expertise for effectiveness. Mistakes are bound to happen to people and within organizations we are all imperfect. Yet, it is how we respond to missteps, corrections, and even failures that often define a leader's legacy. This book explores the role of leaders in a multitude of scenarios to examine how they succeeded and failed in their respective spheres of influence with the hope that we can each learn and grow in our own leadership style. The proverb, "Nana korobi, ya oki" which means "Fall down seven times, stand up eight" is evident throughout this book as we all work to never lose hope as we each pursue our God-given calling.

Lori Chambers MBA
Regional Representative - Birmingham
hopeinternational.org

"Leadership is one of the most important disciplines in Christendom; much of what God desires to accomplish through his church is contingent upon the leadership in the local church. In her book, Linda Dougherty shares stories of leaders in churches, non-profit and business organizations and their lessons learned about failure and recovery. Her composition depicts how recovery and success is possible with hard work and change; it leaves the reader with practical, proven principles that, if adhered to, can improve and enrich any organization.

Dr. Maxie Miller Jr.
Lead Pastor, New City Church of Plant City
Adjunct Professor, Baptist College of Florida

As a student of leadership who has known both success and failure I found Linda's book to be a refreshing addition to the leadership conversation. Her work goes below the surface to probe the inner life of a leader and its implications for our leadership.

TJ Addington
Addington Consulting

A dominate theme in the Bible is that of recovery from failure in the lives of even God's chosen leaders. Linda Dougherty has written a biblically insightful book, beautifully illustrated by inspiring life stories of recovery. Read this book and you will learn that failure need not be final in our lives and those we love and lead.

Jay Brinson, Leader of S.O.A.R.
Serving One Another Resources
http://soargroup.org

I highly recommend this book. The author was my student while she earned her PhD at LBU and this was her dissertation project. It is easy reading but filled with many life experiences and tons of wisdom. You will enjoy it but will also learn from it. Once you start reading it you will not want to lay it down.

Dr. Neal Weaver
Chancellor
Louisiana Baptist University

Copyright © 2021 by Linda Dougherty

ISBN: 978-1-947153-23-3

Critical Mass Books
Davenport, Florida

www.criticalmasspublishing.com

Cover Design   Eowyn Riggins
Interior Layout Rachel Greene

To the Light of the world who renewed my heart
To Jaz, JW and Aaron who filled the cracks in my heart

Acknowledgements

I am blessed to have great a great family, friends, teachers, and leaders in my life, full of wisdom and knowledge. They have walked with me through difficult times, shared their knowledge, taught valuable lessons, and encouraged me. I'm grateful to all and acknowledge a few:

- My husband, Joe, for love, support, and encouragement
- My Dad, for lessons about working hard and doing my best
- Dr. Gerald Simmons for the spiritual toolkit forty years ago

- Lillian, my friend, surrogate Mom and living example of grace
- Craig Ford for the silly, wonderful story about the Coke bottle
- Three Steve's for the gifts of time, wisdom and discovery
- Brother Blue, a living example of Christian life and leadership

"This too shall pass."
— *Brother Blue*

"For our light and momentary troubles are achieving for us an eternal glory that far outweighs them all. So, we fix our eyes not on what is seen, but on what is unseen, since what is seen is temporary, but what is unseen is eternal."
— *2 Cor 4:17-18 (NIV)*

Contents

Preface i

Introduction 3

Chapter One: What is a Leader? 15

Chapter Two: What is Leadership? 35

Chapter Three: What Should It Look Like? 53

Chapter Four: Are Leaders Made or Born? 71

Chapter Five: Knowing and Leading Yourself 89

Chapter Six: Leadership Credibility 109

Chapter Seven: What is Failure? 123

Chapter Eight: What is Success? 145

Chapter Nine: Organizational Failure and Recovery 163

Chapter Ten: Personal Failure and Recovery 195

Chapter Eleven: Self Discovery is Painful 227

Chapter Twelve: Loss and Recovery 247

Chapter Thirteen: Leading with Integrity 259

Chapter Fourteen: The Riddle of Experience v Memory 269

Closing Thoughts 277

Reference Notes 288

Preface

This book is about leadership and what it looks like from various perspectives. It is about success and failure, with both traditional and alternate definitions. These are stories of people, with their own unique circumstances that provide insight and valuable lessons from their mistakes, failures, and recovery. It is about how we learn to lead *ourselves* before we lead others. Leadership begins on the inside long before it is activated on the outside.

Leadership on the inside starts with our individual moral compass and the values we hold dear. Each leader has gifts, talents, flaws, and quirks. Some have skeletons hidden in the shadows. The way leaders respond to their dreams coming true is a great part of what defines leadership and especially, legacy.

And how they act when dreams come crashing down from the pressures of life, obstacles, and temptation. How leaders treat themselves and others, handle success and failure, develop resiliency, and learn from their mistakes, are all part of how they are able—or not—to get back in the game.

The stories presented here are about people who have risen to success, then failed, and ultimately recovered. We'll examine the reasons for those failures, as well as the path to recovery. Several of the profiles are from friends—leaders who shared their own inspiring stories with me. I greatly appreciate their honesty and vulnerability.

Those who step into the role of leader choose, whether they fully know it or not, to practice what we might call the art of leadership. Dwight D. Eisenhower, the 34th President of the United States, and hero of D-Day in World War II, once said: "Leadership is the art of getting someone else to do something you want done because he wants to do it. Leadership comes from patience and conciliation."[1] It's about using influence, persuasion, wisdom, and credibility to earn and keep the trust of followers.

An example of this is the quadrennial election cycle. Incumbents and candidates use their influence and persuasion to earn—or retain—the confidence of prospective voters based on how credible they are perceived to be.

During the most recent election cycle, there was much negativity and turmoil as part of the process of selecting a viable candidate to run against the incumbent President. It was easy to get overwhelmed by the vast amount of negative information presented in the 24/7 news cycle. Candidates and their platforms were examined to see if they were reasonable, affordable, and even possible. The life of each candidate was also important as a picture of their integrity and credibility is revealed. The idea was to see if they kept their promises, how they voted on key issues, how they served their constituents, if they owned or excused their mistakes and failures, and what they did to correct them.

Failure occurs when leaders do not know what to do or *how* to do it. Great leaders tend to be life-long students, learning from the mistakes of others as they strive to improve and refine their skills. My hope for this book is that it will be a fruitful and beneficial resource, something worthy of the investment of your time. If, though what I have written, you are able to avoid some of the mistakes and failures others have made, then my efforts will have been successful!

> *Some of us learn from other people's mistakes,*
> *The rest of us have to be the other people.*
> *Remember that failure is an event, not a person.*
> *— Zig Ziglar*

"Getting up and moving forward is a choice."
— Zig Ziglar

"Failure isn't fatal, but failure to change might be."
— John Wooden

Introduction

Everybody fails. No one is immune. We humans are frail and mess things up every day. Many of these failures are small and inconsequential. We wouldn't really call them failures, more like minor annoyances, things like burnt toast, spilt milk, torn jeans, lost keys, forgotten email, or that email we forgot to return. The kids get upset about the toast because it tastes bad even after you've scraped off the carbon and apply copious amounts of *Nutella*. They gleefully romp through the milk puddle, making milky footprints all over the kitchen floor. They are delighted about the torn jeans and irked that you made them wait because you took an extra five minutes to send that forgotten email. These are the kinds of thing we would call insignificant.

Sometimes we fail to pay attention while driving, resulting in a failure in the form of a fender bender or yet another ding in the back bumper. Forget to pay a bill on time and incur a late fee. Bleach the whites with a one red shirt and find your husband and son in revolt because they refuse to wear the slightly pink-tinged T-shirts and underwear. No matter that you remind them that no one will ever see them.

All minor stuff, but still no big deal.

But failures can be more serious, like forgetting to pick up Jazz from robotics camp or when she forgets to tell you she needs 20 cupcakes for a party—tomorrow. You are a wife, mom, mentor, and a project leader at work. You are very busy and dedicated, trying to return the last client phone call while driving home from work. The phone slips out of your hand, you become distracted trying to pick it up and the unintentional, accidental, and unthinkable life-changing horror happens.

You wake up in the hospital and the police officer says, "you are under arrest for distracted driving and vehicular negligence resulting in serious bodily injuries." Other people in the accident are seriously wounded. You are stone cold sober and till, because you were a distracted driver and you have caused other people to suffer disabling and disfiguring injuries. You are not going home tonight, nor are you going back to work tomorrow. Jazz is still at school, waiting and worried, there are no cupcakes to be made, and your immediate future is at Central Booking.

And the worst is yet to come.

Some might call this a preventable failure. You intentionally chose to make the call, but you could have waited until you pulled over, arrived at home, or even until the next morning. If you ask yourself after the fact, "What is the worst thing that would have happened if I chose not to return that call until tomorrow?", the answer is likely a mild reprimand from your boss or maybe a slightly miffed client. But in retrospect that would have been the better, certainly safer choice.

We are faced with choices like this every day. Asking ourselves questions is a good way to assess the risk and so is giving up the idea that it could never happen to you. After all, it's just a minute—one short call.

Every day, *good people with no intention of harming anyone*, make bad choices which result in horrible consequences. No one intends to cause a terrible automobile accident or embezzle Little League funds, leave the baby in a hot car, or poison the neighbor's cat when they discard a tiny bit of leftover antifreeze in the flowerbed. We do not intend to cause harm, but we do. Sometimes it is a just a bad mistake, and sometimes it is an unintended, but nevertheless criminal action. However, ignorance of the law is not always a valid defense.

We failed to obey the law.

Recovering from failure can take a few minutes, a few days, or in some cases, a lifetime. The passengers in the other car, the victims of the distracted driver, were physically injured and disabled. Whether the at-fault driver was distracted, impaired or exhausted, the result is still horrible. The victims' injuries prevent them from returning immediately to work, resulting in a loss of income and things like late car and mortgage payments. But it's not their fault.

Wise planning on their part to have an emergency fund would mitigate the financial crisis, but yet, they suffer this burden not of their making. They will still be recovering physically, emotionally, and financially when you leave prison and the civil court case is settled.

Long-term emotional trauma is also the result of poor choices. Infidelity, (cheating) or an emotional affair on *Facebook* can cost dearly and impact the marital relationship, sometimes for a lifetime.

When our family consulted an attorney for estate planning, we engaged in some casual chitchat as we waited for the documents to be printed. He said his business had increased quite a bit since *Facebook* became so popular. It seems a lot of unhappy married couples look up old boyfriends and girlfriends, reconnect with them secretly and start having affairs. The evidence is all hiding in plain sight right there on

Facebook for the judge and the world to see. No one was meant to be hurt, but here we are knee deep in divorce, dividing Aunt Mabel's antiques and fighting a custody battle for the kids and the mutual funds.

There are times when we know exactly what we are doing—we *want and intend* to do it. Being passed over for the promotion was humiliating and hurtful. We feel anger and have the urge for revenge. A false sense of entitlement has rusted the moral compass and bad decisions are sure to follow. We become angry and key the manager's *Mercedes*. He makes a lot of money and takes the credit for our work. We deserved that promotion. This intentional and malicious act would haunt most people. The better choice is to seek information from your manager, accept constructive criticism, and work hard to improve opportunities for future advancement.

In each scenario, an accident, a divorce, or the damaged Mercedes paint-job, things escalate and become devastating. I was never supposed to happen this way or go this far awry. We never meant to get caught. No one was supposed to be injured or hospitalized, but they were. The camera in the parking garage recorded the damage to the *Mercedes*. We wish to change those childish actions, the angry, biting words, but now there are severe consequences. How did we get here? Can we find our way back?

Is there a way to redemption and recovery?

There is indeed a path to redemption, restoration, and a better future if you are willing to be truthful with yourself and others. There is hard work to do, starting with an answer to the question, "How did we get here?" Recovery may include making restitution, time in jail, probation, and other corrective measures. Despite all of this, there are many powerful examples of people who followed the difficult and humbling path to recovery and a highly successful future.

Alan K. Simpson was a self-described "monster" in high school, assaulting other students, torching an abandoned federal property, and committing many other crimes. He was arrested after damaging equipment owned by the U.S. government, and he served two years' probation and paid restitution. Sometime later, following employment in various vocations, Mr. Simpson was elected as a United States Congressman from the Wyoming and later as a Senator. He rose to become Republican majority whip from 1985 to 1995, working to assist Senate Leader Bob Dole. He was reportedly considered as a potential vice-presidential candidate by George H. W. Bush.

Simpson found redemption, but he had to work long and hard for it after making some deliberately poor choices. In his own words, he and his friends "went out to do damage and raise hell." He said years later, "My probation officer always believed in my capacity for redemption, even when my actions did not inspire confidence."[1] It's a great redemption story.

Redemption means to atone for a mistake, or restore, make good, or buy back, just as stocks and bonds that can be sold with a "redemption clause" from the seller. This enables them to buy back their stocks which increases their value. One person's reputation can be worth billions of dollars. Proverbs 22:1 says, *"A good name is more desirable than great riches; to be esteemed is better than silver or gold."*

But sometimes recovery takes a long time and a lot of change.

Papa John's Pizza founder, John Schnatter, is an example of what happens when a reputation is severely damaged and when a firm connects their brand too closely to one person. Mr. Schnatter used very insulting and derogatory language on a public conference call, tarnishing his reputation and by extension, that of the company. The turmoil that followed created a huge set of problems for *Papa John's*. The firm lost the position of being "official pizza supplier" to the NFL and stock value fell by a third. The brand was weakened and became vulnerable to takeover attempts. The CEO and Chairman of the Board resigned.[2] More than two years later, the pizza chain is still recovering, and some franchises are still down 20% or more in sales. Our choices and words have weight and impact, sometimes in the billions of dollars.

It is also important to understand what redemption is *not*. It is not allowing a recovering alcoholic, who was arrested for DUI, to drive a school bus or church van, even after being released from jail. It is not asking that same recovering alcoholic to work as a bartender or brew master. Media journalist Jane Velez-Mitchell humorously says, "Redemption isn't giving a bank robber a job as a teller."[3]

Those who love of the *Star Wars* legacy and the moral lessons embedded within the themes of its storyline will appreciate this reference to the *redemption* of Darth Vader. In the movie, *The Return of the Jedi*, Vader died as a hero when he finally remembered who he was and that there was still good in him. Anakin Skywalker, Jedi knight, became the villain Darth Vader, but after spending most of his life on the Dark Side, he repented just before his death. He helped his son, Luke Skywalker, escape from the Emperor's Force.[4]

Vader experienced redemption in the storyline, the kind that resembles historical accounts in the Bible. Redemption is, in fact, also a religious concept, where one is redeemed/saved from sin and evil to regain or be restored to one's former status.

King Nebuchadnezzar's story is one of redemption and restoration. It's found in the Book of Daniel in the Bible.

I am a Christian, so this book is being written with a Biblical perspective in mind. But I am also a frail human being subject to sin and temptation. I have failed often in my life, sometimes miserably so by speaking unkind words, and being mean, petty, or arrogant. My cutting words and angry deeds were not an example of a loving and humble Christian. We strive to be good Ambassadors and represent our Father well, however, Christians are not immune from making poor choices, speaking ugly words, or from the lure of sin. We bear the serious consequences of our words and deeds just like anyone else.

A Christian is an ordinary person, who has accepted the extraordinary sacrifice of God's grace at Calvary. Romans 3:23-24 speaks of redemption as Christians believe: *"for all have sinned and fall short of the glory of God, and all are justified freely by his grace through the redemption that came by Christ Jesus."* Christians believe it is through divine providence that we breath, love, work, and experience life in all its joy and pain, sadness, awe, disappointment, pleasure, satisfaction, and optimism. We believe in second and third chances.

Most of us admit that we need them every day.

Christians believe anyone can chose to recover from failure, learn and grow from it, and move forward to a measure of success. It is often difficult, and takes time, patience, and lots of hard work, but it is possible. From the Biblical perspective, nothing is impossible with God. Mercy, grace, and redemption are readily available, but we still must get up and deal with the often messy residue from our failures. The natural consequences must play out, sometimes for a protracted period of time. When failure knocks you down it is important to *choose* to get back up and move forward.

> *"Getting up and moving forward is a choice.*
> *Many of life's failures are people who did not realize*
> *how close they were to success when they gave up."*
> — *Zig Ziglar*

"Ultimately, a leader is not judged so much by how well he or she leads, but by how well he or she serves."
— *Kevin Cashman, CEO at Korn Ferry*

"What am I building that lasts?"
— *Barack Obama*

Chapter One: What is a Leader?

Sarge? Boss? Leader of the pack? The sign posted on our youth pastor's door read, "If nobody is following, then you are just taking a walk." This quote is often attributed to John Maxwell, civil rights attorney and Baptist minister the Rev. Benjamin L. Hooks and others.[1] According to the leadership expert, Professor Peter F. Drucker, a leader in the most basic form is "someone with followers."[2] How's that for clarity?

But just how does that "someone" acquire followers to become a leader?

In a word: Influence. Best-selling author Chuck Swindoll says, "Leadership is influence that inspires." This occurs when a person has influence on, or authority over others.

This can happen in many ways, from friendly persuasion—winning the confidence of the voters in free societies— to the use of threats of physical violence or actual use of force in totalitarian police states such as China or Venezuela. But at that point, any real leadership has devolved into destructive authoritarianism.

Having followers is, of course, a very important part of being a leader. Barry Z. Posner, Accolti Endowed Professor of Leadership at the *Leavey School of Business* at Santa Clara University in California has a fantastic *TED Talk* delivered at the University of Nevada. He asked, "Why would anybody follow you? Why would anybody pay attention to you?" His conclusion was one word: Credibility. He said, "we follow people we believe are credible—competent, honest, forward-thinking, and inspirational. People will not believe the message, if they don't believe the messenger."[3] So a leader is a person with credibility. Dictators and other authoritarian type leaders do not use credibility; they use force and terror. Such things are perhaps effective to a point, but true inspiring leadership is benevolent, not brutal.

Effective and benevolent leaders generally have credibility, knowledge, and expertise. They use their influence with those who follow them. They gain permission to lead, earn respect, and loyalty from their followers, which they then use to guide and coach their followers' ideas, choices, and actions. Good leaders recognize the need for change and use positive means to persuade their constituents toward new ideas and compelling goals.

This can have a profound and lasting effect.

One example is how Mary Gates, mother of billionaire tech titan Bill Gates, convinced him to use his good fortune to help others. Mary was the first female chairwoman of the national *United Way* board. She had experience in finance, philanthropy, and funding community needs. She used her influence, albeit in a persistent and unusual way, to convince her very busy CEO son, Bill, to donate generously to the *United Way*. It was "a letter that his mother gave his bride-to-be at the time in 1994 that lead to his work in philanthropy on a purposeful scale. Her letter read: 'From those to whom much is given, much is expected.' Six months later, she died. Gates never forgot her words."[4]

We are all aware of the vast amount of good work that has come from the *Bill and Melinda Gates Foundation*. They are funding research looking for cures for diseases such as AIDS and malaria, and many other medical, educational, and cultural issues are being addressed. The *Gates Foundation* provides funding, measures results, makes changes, and moves forward. They use what works and discard what doesn't.

In other words, they practice benevolent and effective leadership.

A word of caution: *An effective leader is not always a great moral leader.* Sadly, history is filled with examples of gifted leaders who brought out the worst in their followers. The Italian Fascist dictator Benito Mussolini was an effective leader in the 1920s and 1930s. In fact, he famously made the trains run on time. But those efficient trains later transported thousands of Jewish people from Italy to the Auschwitz death camp in southern Poland during the Second World War.[5] Mussolini, or "Il Duce" as he was called (literally means, "the leader") was effective, but evil.

Great moral leaders, on the other hand, seek to elevate the individual or organization, improve the circumstances of all in their sphere of influence. Mary Gates did this graciously and well, employing great moral leadership to accomplish tremendous benefits for humanity. And she knew that pursuing funding from her son and future daughter-in-law would make a huge difference in countless lives.

When she died in 1994, she was eulogized by University of Washington President William Gerberding as having "infectious, effervescent joy," and a "largeness of purpose and spirit. She was a luminous presence and a powerful influence at this University and in the community."

I suspect that the joy she experienced came from serving others and seeing the results of that service. She was evidentially a charismatic person, remembered and honored even sixteen years after her death for being a "powerful influence." In October 2010, the *Mary M. Gates Learning Center at United Way Worldwide* in Alexandria, VA was dedicated by her son and other family members. The center is dedicated to her memory, "in honor of the late Mary M. Gates, who provided leadership in volunteering, advocacy and giving for *United Way* on a local, national and international level. The Center is built on Mrs. Gates' belief that learning, sharing, and working together will make the world a better place."[6] She was indeed charismatic and kind, using her influence for human and benevolent works.

Of course, *charisma* is not always an indicator of great moral leadership. Adolf Hitler was, by all accounts, very charismatic. He was revered as "Der Fuhrer" ("the leader") by his willing followers who thrilled at his captivating, though poisonous speeches. But his was a brutal and authoritarian kind of charisma.

Winston Churchill, on the other hand—also a man with a flair for communication—used his gifts for noble and benevolent purposes. Even when he was far from actual power and in the political wilderness, he was someone who could persuade crowds. And when he became Prime Minister in May of 1940, he brought that charisma to the world stage at a crucial time in the history of Western Civilization. President John F. Kennedy, when he made Churchill an honorary citizen of the

United States in 1963, quoted Edward R. Murrow's line that the great Englishman "mobilized the English language and sent it into battle."

The contrast between Churchill and Hitler couldn't be more stark. Hitler was malevolent. Churchill was benevolent. Consider these uplifting words from the Briton:

> *"It is always an error in diplomacy to press a matter when it is quite clear that no further progress is to be made. It is also a great error if you ever give the impression abroad that you are using language which is more concerned with your domestic politics than with the actual fortunes and merits of the various great countries upon the Continent to whom you offer advice."*[7]

The moral compasses of these two effective leaders were studies in contrast. Their leadership styles were diametrically different. And their ultimate goals were polar opposites. This shows the stark difference between an immoral leader and a moral one. Consider these dark and repressive words from Hitler:

> *"the sacred mission of the German people…to assemble and preserve the most valuable racial elements…and raise them to the dominant position." "All who are not of a good race are chaff,"* wrote Hitler. *It was necessary for*

Germans to "occupy themselves not merely with the breeding of dogs, horses, and cats but also with care for the purity of their own blood." He "ascribed international significance to the elimination of Jews, which…must necessarily be a bloody process"[8]

Moving from history to more current events, we can find another example of this contrast between good and evil in the horror and turmoil in Venezuela being fomented by its disputed leader, President Nicolas Madura. "Venezuela is really a dictatorship," says Julieta Lopez, aunt of the jailed opposition leader Leopoldo López. "We have a facade of democracy."[9]

In 2017, Ms. Lopez told a journalist from *Reuters* journalist, "There is no right to express a different political opinion without being threatened, beaten, or imprisoned."[10] Dictators follow a common path, one unaffected by historical context or geography. Greed, love of power, and corrupt values are a despot's hallmarks, as well as those of the minions who follow.

Leopoldo Lopez was released from prison in April 2019, and as of September 2019, was residing at the Spanish Embassy in the capital of Caracas, awaiting ascendance to the presidency should Maduro step down—or be removed. Lopez is, in fact, recognized by the parliamentary president Juan

Guaido, as the legitimate and true President of Venezuela. Guaido, in turn, is recognized as the transitional head of state by the United States and more than fifty other countries. He is moving forward toward installing Mr. Lopez as soon as possible. Negotiations are in process between Maduro's party and the Lopez party, but no definitive results have been accomplished as of this writing.

President Donald Trump invited Mr. Guaido to the 2020 State of the Union address, meeting with him at the White House earlier that day. In response to this, six *Citgo* oil executives, who were originally arrested by Maduro forces in 2017 and later released to house arrest, were then rearrested and moved to a prison site. Five of these executives are U.S. Citizens, and one is a permanent resident. The State Department has been working toward their release since they were first arrested, but now it is even more doubtful they will be returned to the US any time soon.[11]

Who is a Leader?

Most great leaders are not rich, famous, glamorous, or privileged. They are ordinary people with extraordinary hearts who possess some measure of talent that can be cultivated. Their hearts are geared toward a deep and sincere desire to make a real difference. This may be a product of their upbringing, or from observing and experiencing life's up and downs, or reading about great leaders of the past and present, or all of the above. Most leaders share some common attributes and qualities but sometimes use their talent and time for less-than-positive results.

Being a leader can be quite impactful even when there is only one singular follower. I recall a story about a leader named Drew who serves one person, a young lady permanently impacted by his humor, kindness, and care. We have no idea what kind of specific influence she will have on her fellow humans, but we can be assured that it will be excellent, positive, and uplifting. Effective leadership has a ripple effect that tends to work exponentially, even for years to come.

Sometimes we do not recognize ourselves as leaders because we do not see the bigger picture or believe we must be leading multiple people in a group or organization to qualify. But, one person may indeed lead another person with great impact.

Being a leader is like owning a car, or a gun, or a paintbrush. We choose how to wield leadership for good or evil, or for personal gain or service to others. This makes the difference. A man with a car can drive himself to work, or drive to pick up his neighbor, thus serving himself, his neighbor, and society. He earns his paycheck, his neighbor gets to work and earn his paycheck, and the carbon footprint caused by his neighbor driving to work is diminished. He uses his car to serve and elevate his neighbor and, by extension, society as a whole. His neighbor may barter or pay him for transport, and that transaction has an economic benefit in a free enterprise system.

The same thinking holds true with the gun or the paintbrush and the choice of how they are used. If I shoot a poisonous snake in my neighbor's yard (local ordinances considered, of course) it serves him well by eliminating a deadly threat. Lending him my paintbrush will help him paint his fence. If he steals my paintbrush, and I shoot him, he is relegated to a hospital bed, or the morgue, and I go to jail. Members of society are then paying for my room, board, medical care, and other amenities, and I am not serving them or myself well. Leaders choose how they will serve their followers and how they will use opportunities for leadership.

One person, practicing the art of leadership in a meaningful and positive way, can have great influence and make a deep impact on us. That can happen even if we never meet the leader in person. These individuals may be identified as "thought leaders" or "influencers." These are people who have special knowledge, expertise, and/or influence and are recognized as such in their communities or vocational fields.

Some local leaders and influencers who have had a positive impact on me are:

- Liam, a retired senior leader, executive, and mentor
- Joseph H. Dougherty, my late father-in-law and a sergeant in the Army
- Craig Ford, a former missionary and current pastor at Church of Christ in Billings, Montana
- Michael Loewy, economics professor extraordinaire

These fine leaders have strongly influenced my thoughts, challenged my ideas and choices, and have impacted my life in positive and substantial ways. To me, they are giants, and I am grateful for their tutelage, as well as for the opportunities they have afforded me.

Two famous people who have influenced me in a most positive manner are:

- Dave Ramsey, a radio personality and founder of *Financial Peace University*
- Walter Williams, a syndicated columnist and lauded economics professor

Though I have never had the privilege of meeting him, Dr. Williams—the John M. Olin Distinguished Professor of Economics at George Mason University in Fairfax, Virginia—he has influenced me greatly. Along with his academic work, he is a best-selling author, speaker, radio personality, and SME (subject matter expert) in the areas of common sense, personal liberty, and the power of government. He has sat in for various talk radio hosts, including Rush Limbaugh, since the early 1990s.

Dr. Williams is an elegant, yet plain-spoken and brilliant, communicator. He was a major influence for my choice of major for my undergraduate degree—Economics. A man of deep honesty, to the point of being very blunt, he makes people uncomfortable on occasion. But that's okay, we all need a nudge toward reality in order for us to stretch and grow—to learn "*adulting*," the millennial's term of choice for what used to be called, simply, growing up.

It is notable that Dr. Williams spent some of his childhood in public housing in a single parent home and was drafted into the Army in 1959. For an African-American, that was a difficult period in history, and the dynamics of that turbulent time period could have pointed Dr. Williams toward a life of trouble. But he chose another path—one of wisdom. It was the right choice and brought him great success as he used education to better his lot in life. Sharing humorous and entertaining stories about his life experiences, using factual and bone-dry humor in his unique manner, he is able to connect with almost everyone.

Personally, he challenges my ideas and encourages me to change and grow through constant reading, studying, and learning. He advocates engaging in, and protecting, free market capitalism, as well as recognizing optimum financial and business opportunities when they present themselves.

Dr. Williams delivered the following remarks to an audience in Irvington, New York, on June 28, 2014 at the *Foundation for Economic Education* meeting:

> *"Capitalism, or what some call free markets, is relatively new in human history. Prior to capitalism, the way individuals amassed great wealth was by looting, plundering, and enslaving their fellow man. With the rise of capitalism, it became possible to amass great wealth by serving and pleasing your fellow man. Capitalists seek to discover what people want and produce and market it as efficiently as possible as a means to profit."[12]*

Dr. Williams passed away on December 2, 2020. His deep influence will live on, as we remember his dry humor, sharp wit and his love and vigilant defense of personal liberty. He often measured the affect and usefulness of a legislative action, government policy or regulation by asking if it will result in more liberty or less liberty?

Dr. Thomas Sowell sums it up very well, "Walter, a professor of economics at George Mason University for 40 years, once said he hoped that, on the day he died, he would have taught a class that day. And that is just the way it was when he died Wednesday, Dec. 2. He was my best friend for half a century. There was no one I trusted more or whose integrity I respected more."[13]

As an example of success in the arena of capitalism, consider *Zappos*, *Amazon*, and *HM Fashion*. These companies use constant disruption, innovation, agility, and high performing staff to perfect the art of customer service with the goal of cultivating happy customers and repeat business.

The opposite side of the coin is illustrated by many tragic events occurring in recent years. We see an impressionable young person trying to emulate an admired public figure (thought leader). Musicians, movie stars, media artists, and athletes who move from humble means to suddenly great wealth are often seen as winners, heroes, and role models. Because they wield such tremendous influence (a foundation of leadership) their fans (followers) attempt to replicate their speech, fashion, behavior, and lifestyle. Sports and music celebrities are personified as larger than life, and when viewed by immature young people it sometimes turns out negative.

Mark Walton, former running back for the University of Miami, was raised mostly by his mother. His father died when he was in elementary school, and his mother died a few years ago. He was arrested three times in South Florida in early 2019 for various driving infractions, weapons charges, and other assorted crimes. He was originally with the *Cincinnati Bengals*, signing with them right out of college—a contract worth about $3.5 million dollars. He was later waived by the team, perhaps because of his erratic behavior and criminal activities.

Walton was then picked up by Coach Brian Flores of the *Miami Dolphins* who said, "Everyone deserves a second chance," when signing him. This second chance was after he was arrested in Miami for DUI in early 2019. The *Dolphins* put him on the team in May 2019 for about $500,000.[14] He was due to be back on the field by December 2nd, however, he was cut from the team after being arrested for domestic violence. He allegedly shoved and punched a pregnant woman after she told him she was pregnant.

As of January 2020, he was under arrest for a second alleged domestic violence charge.[15] Walton has clearly squandered some tremendous opportunities because of poor choices and his clear lack of self-control. We look at celebrities, actors, athletes, and artists as leaders, heroes, superstars, and, yes, role models. Most of them are well paid for their work, earning great sums of money for endorsing products and services on television, *Twitter*, or *Instagram*.

Another type of leader is what we call a "social influencer," someone who persuades others to use a product or service. One of the most famous social influencers is Kim Kardashian, who dominates social media platforms such as *Twitter* and

Instagram. She has held steady at #13 on the Twitter scale for nearly a decade. She is famous for being, well, famous, I suppose. In 2012, she commanded $10,000[16] for an endorsement, $250,000[17] for another in 2017, and a cool half million for yet another in 2019.[18]

In fairness, while Kim Kardashian may be, at times, a highly controversial influencer, she does lend her celebrity status to some worthwhile causes. She is a volunteer at the *Children's Hospital* of Los Angeles, has participated in ventures for the *Make-A-Wish Foundation*, and has donated generously to the *Lurie Children's Hospital* in Chicago. She and her family contributed to the *Red Cross* and *Salvation Army* in relief efforts in Houston after Hurricane Harvey. She has raised awareness--and sympathy—for victims of human trafficking, as well as those who suffer from mental health issues and physical ailments.

More recently, she has worked within the criminal justice system, even influencing President Donald Trump's decision to show compassion for individuals such as Alice Marie Johnson, a former federal prisoner. Mrs. Johnson was convicted of cocaine trafficking in 1996 and sentenced to life behind bars. The President commuted her sentence in 2019, and in August of 2020, he granted her a full pardon. She has become a leader in her own right, using her time in prison to become an ordained minister and now devotes her life to criminal justice reform. She credits her release and pardon as divine intervention.

Kim suffers from the itchy, splotchy skin condition called *psoriasis*. She has even shared some candid photographs of an outbreak of red and scaly areas on her skin, including her face.[19] This is a huge step, because she makes her living as a fashion, makeup, and lifestyle influencer, a world in which everything is about appearance and image. It certainly took courage and humility to put herself out like that. And she has positively impacted hundreds of young people who suffer from the same condition.

I had the great privilege of meeting Dave Ramsey during a four-day seminar in 2001 in Brentwood, TN. He taught our group about leadership, entrepreneurship, financial pitfalls, and credit and debt solutions. His *Financial Peace University* model is truly a way to change your legacy and your family tree. If you follow the program it *will* change your life. He is a credible (not to mention, *in*credible) leader, a man of integrity, and is known for holding his followers accountable. Dave motivates his followers. People listen to him, even thousands who have never met him. With the bold honesty, tempered by compassion and mercy, he tells his callers: "We buy things we don't need, with money we don't have, to impress people we don't like. Let's quit that."[20]

Most of us will never meet the leaders and influencers who impact our lives by the products or services they offer, the decisions they make, the words they speak, or the actions they take. For our political leaders, history records how they handle the success of winning an election and if it their service was beneficial, detrimental, or of little impact.

For business leaders, the economy, job market, and paychecks are affected by their influence. Leaders of technology, media, and science impact us each day through innovation, information, medicine, liberty, and quality (and length) of life.

John Maxwell says, "Everything rises and falls on leadership." It really matters. And we cannot fully envision all of the many ways it may touch our lives. It is extremely important that each person who assumes the role of a leader be fully aware of how they may affect the lives and fortunes of others. It is not a role for the weak, selfish, arrogant, or decidedly evil person. It takes vision, confidence, humility, integrity, and grit to lead well and impact the world in the most positive and beneficial way.

"Leadership is a choice, not a position."
— Steven Covey

"Leadership is about making others better as a result of your presence and making sure that impact lasts in your absence."
— Sheryl Sandberg

Chapter Two: What is Leadership?

Dwight D. Eisenhower said, "Leadership is the art of getting someone else to do something you want done because he wants to do it."[1] In his classic book, *On Becoming a Leader*, Warren Bennis, defines leadership as, "...the capacity to translate vision into reality." He also wrote, "To an extent, leadership is like beauty: It's hard to define, but you know it when you see it."[2] And in his bestselling book, *The 360 Degree Leader*, John Maxwell says, "Leadership is influence—nothing more, nothing less."

Peter Drucker, Warren Bennis, and John Maxwell are highly-regarded experts on the subject of leadership. They know it is much more than the benign definitions and theories found in textbooks. But frankly, it is sometimes helpful to look at those definitions, as well as the etymology of words to understand any subject—especially leadership.

According to *Dictionary.com*, "ship" is a suffix—a letter or group of letters added to a noun to establish status or condition. In this case, "ship" is a *noun* suffix, to show the position or function of a leader.[3]

1. Indicating the qualities belonging to a class or group of people, e.g., craftsmanship.
2. Indicating office or profession, e.g., ambassadorship.

So, we expect a leader to be someone with knowledge—even expertise—about leadership, having developed specific qualities, and then translating all of this into skillful practice. This moves someone from the mere practice of leadership—which can often be circumstantial—into the *art* of leadership. As in sports or medicine, practice gives way to improvement, and one becomes better and better over time.

Of course, the practice of leadership and the *art* of leadership are two very different things. Leaders starts by learning and then practicing their skills over time, which allows them to grow into being craftsmen. A craftsman is one who uses the tools of a trade in a refined and skillful manner; sometimes referred to as a "master" of his trade. My father was a master carpenter in his day. I remember when he cut down a

Florida cherry tree. He took it to the sawmill. Later, he planed a piece and used it to make a picture frame for me. Our neighbor, Mr. Leon, works in grand old homes, replicating pieces for paneling, mantels, and other woodworking wonders. Mr. Leon says it takes many years to understand the nuances and subtle tweaks to get the best out of a piece of walnut or cherry.

John Baldoni, a Top 100 leadership speaker, describes the process this way: "The practice of leadership is setting the right example, providing vision and guidance, and doing all that is necessary for people in the organization to succeed. The really hard part, the *art* of leadership, is knowing what to do, and when, why, and how to do it."[4]

My husband and I love to watch cooking shows and we always learn new techniques and recipes to try. It takes us a long time to make a dish look like the television chef version––and whether it tastes like it is anyone's guess. Chefs like Emeril Lagasse, Jacques Pepin, or Lidia Bastianich will tell you that they started off by watching other people cook. Then, they did the hard work of studying, watching, learning, and chopping as an apprentice, and doing it over and over again. And now it looks easy. They may not admit how many times they burned food, cut their fingers, or ruined a recipe. But they learned through hard work, diligent trial and error and, after much effort and practice, they "mastered" their craft. Now they know what to do, when, why, and how.

They make the culinary arts look simple and easy. Some of them lead organizations that have restaurants, produce television shows, publish books, and book personal appearances. It takes years of hard work, dedication to their craft, and refining of their skills. Chef Lidia Bastianich says, "I've been a cook all my life, but I am still learning to be a good chef."[5] My husband and I had the pleasure of dining at *Felidia*, one of her flagship restaurants in New York City. It was a three-hour experience, but well worth the time and expense for this once-in-a-lifetime event. The ambiance of the restaurant was fabulous, the level of service from the service staff was superb, and the texture and taste of the food was fantastic. It was all a testament to Ms. Bastianich's leadership and her devotion to high standards and consistent quality.

To me, leadership is a learned art, full of nuances—the nooks and crannies of personalities and emotional needs—and knowing the best way to do the right thing at the right time. It is also a practice, like medicine or dentistry, based on scientific, sociological, and other academic influences, plus emotional intelligence, common sense, and a humble and teachable attitude. You can become a great leader over time, as you learn the science and develop the art.

There are many applications for leadership, where it occurs and how it is lived out. Leaders use persuasion, inspiration, and clear communication of the vision to motivate their followers to perform in a desired manner, while serving, developing, and caring for them. This is the obligation and duty of a true leader.

Returning to Peter Drucker's definition, he later expanded those few simple words ("a leader is someone who has followers") to include his thoughts about the duty of a leader in practicing *the art of being a leader*. He wrote, "Leadership is the lifting of a man's vision to higher sights, the raising of a man's performance to a higher standard, the building of a man's personality beyond its normal limitations."[6] Another leadership expert, John Maxwell, describes his conviction about the extraordinary purpose for his life, "You see, my passion in life is growing and equipping others to do remarkable things and lead significant and fulfilled lives." He wrote this boldly and prominently on his website blog, documenting how he does this, through several organizations he has founded, including *EQUIP* and his *Leadership Foundation*.[7]

Leadership might be considered by some to be a *position* such as held by Amazon CEO Jeff Bezos, politico Joe Biden, or civic and philanthropy leaders Bill and Melinda Gates. For others, it may be a *calling* as a philosophical or religious leader, such as the late Rev. Billy Graham or Michael W. Austin, a scholar-philosopher at Eastern Kentucky University. Each leader, no matter their practice, position or calling, has their own strategy and agenda. They view their leadership practice through their own prism. Whether it is a business, academic, legal, religious, familial, or other leader, each will be viewed differently by those who follow, and those who oppose leaders who have their individual philosophies, beliefs, and methods.[8]

Leadership works best when we have evidence that the person who is leading is truthful, secure, confident, credible, and competent. We must have confidence in their ability to identify problems and challenges, finding ways to solve these problems, improve the situation, and move to a better place. General Colin Powell once said, "Leadership is solving problems. The day soldiers stop bringing you their problems is the day you have stopped leading them. They have either lost confidence that you can help or concluded you do not care. Either case is a failure of leadership."[9]

The world is getting more complex and problems are increasingly difficult and challenging. A good leader is secure enough to surround herself with people who are smarter than she is and have specific knowledge and skills to help solve the resident problems. In the web blog, *A Principal's Reflections*, created by digital thought leader and author Eric Sheninger, he penned an article about teamwork and diversity titled, *"Great Leaders Surround Themselves with Smart People."* He says:

> *Leadership is a team sport. It is not about what one person does, but instead the cumulative actions of everyone in an organization. Sure, a leader has to make some pretty important decisions at times that might require bypassing consensus or collaboration, but those are few and far between when you look at the big picture. Success requires broad embracement of ideas where people are motivated to change because they want to, not necessarily because they are forced to. It's both a two-way street and a give and takes relationship. Effective leaders rely on the expertise of others regardless of where they are in the organizational hierarchy.[10]*

A truly exceptional leader is humble, honest, compassionate, visionary, inspiring, self-confident, unselfish, and can speak the truth with love, grace, and mercy. They desire to help others achieve their potential and seek ways to develop and guide their followers to the next level—whatever that may be. They also possess and develop habits that enhance their ability to lead. They will literally practice leading the way a doctor practices medicine, taking time to diagnose various conditions and situations (bedside manner) and prescribe remedies. Leaders have their own "*deskside* manner," habits cultivated over time in an on-going effort to refine their skills.

It is important to note that while leaders and managers work hand in hand for the good of an organization, managers are not necessarily leaders. Leadership happens when there is willingness on the part followers to listen and consider, entertain ideas, and be open to inspiration toward a goal. Managers follow pre-established policy, processes, and guidelines and, while some great managers become great leaders, not all managers will rise, or even aspire to leadership.

It is entirely possible to be a great manager, but not even a good leader.

Andy Dunn, former CEO of *Bonobos*, a men's retail attire store, said "Leadership is inspiring people. Management is keeping the trains running on time."

Indeed.

Why is Leadership Important?

Michael Hyatt, former CEO of *Thomas Nelson Publishing*, has posed this question in a blog article, "Why Do Leaders Exist?" He wrote, "My answer to the question is this: *Leaders exist to create a shift in reality.* Without leaders, things drift along. They go where they want to go, following the path of least resistance.

However, when this is not desirable—or acceptable—you hire, elect, appoint, or *become* a leader. The leader's job is to overcome resistance and make things flow in a different direction. His or her job is to create a different reality."[11]

I think leaders exist and are needed to help keep society functioning effectively and smoothly, to keep chaos and anarchy at bay, and to allow us to have the opportunity to a peaceful pursuit of life, liberty, and happiness. What we do with that opportunity determines our individual outcomes.

Leadership is important and necessary. In society we are governed by rules and laws and we value role models as examples to help guide our choices and actions in various venues. Business leaders set forth the vision and mission for an enterprise and oversee their departments and divisions with a view toward positive results for the brand, product lines, and services. They also must be engaged to guide the firm toward good social and ecological citizenship, as well as successful financial results, and the wellbeing of employees, stockholders, and consumers.

Our military trains soldiers, sailors, airmen, and marines to follow orders while accomplishing their missions. Military leaders keep order through a chain of command. Imagine a platoon of armed personnel with no clear destination or mission wandering aimlessly around a battlefield. The sheer chaos would result in the loss of morale, effectiveness, and perhaps even lives. I will soon share the story about my father-in-law's experience in World War II—a real-life demonstration of the importance of the chain of command and its key to a mission.

Without inspiring and competent leadership, people tend to wander with no clear goal, destination, or accomplishment. Worse yet, they can become disgruntled and despondent. Ask any parent whether their children need parental leadership and guidance to navigate daily life. Of course they do. They need love, affirmation, healthy emotions, boundaries, accountability—and consequences. Outwardly they may flinch and protest, but most everyone behaves and performs better when they know the boundaries and what is expected of them.

Leaders provide this kind of guidance and clarity.

Whenever there is a leadership void, it will usually be filled by someone with their own ideas, beliefs, and agenda. This can present as either *benevolent* or *malevolent* leadership, such as the ongoing crisis in Venezuela, which has been in a consistent state of turmoil and chaos. The complete cultural meltdown has greatly affected the quality of life for citizens. To complicate matters, rivaling factions of political and judicial parties are in conflict. In the National Assembly, leader, Juan Guaidó is considered the legitimate President. The Supreme Tribunal of Justice champions a different president, Nicholas Maduro, who barely clings to power. With no clear governmental leadership, the citizens suffer from a lack of basic necessities, things like utilities, a steady supply of food, medical care, fuel, and assorted other staples. Crime is rampant and inflation is on the rise. People are fleeing the country, and the banking system is collapsing. Personal liberty is in danger, and the military continues to flex its muscles.

So far, all attempts to remove or displace Nicolas Maduro have failed. "Operation Gideon" was an attempt in May 2020 by a group of armed invaders, including several Americans, to overthrow Maduro. Two Americans were captured and charged with terroristic invasion. They face long prison sentences, with other alleged perpetrators. Legislative elections are scheduled for December 2020 and Maduro, "In an effort to promote 'national reconciliation' and increase voter participation,"[12] has pardoned over 100 opposition leaders, including 20 deputies from the National Assembly who were accused of plotting against Maduro. Twenty-seven opposition groups plan to boycott the election to deny the Socialist Party any shred of legitimacy. The horror of this continuing power struggle is the plight of the Venezuelan people.

In the *Economist's* Bello column—the September 10, 2020 weekly edition—the correspondent for South America summed things up sadly and succinctly, "EVEN BY RECENT abysmal standards, this has been a bad year for Venezuelans. Covid-19 has struck a country whose health system collapsed long ago. Because of mismanagement and, since last year, swinging American sanctions, the economy is sinking to subsistence level: GDP is set to decline by about 15% this year, and will be 72% smaller than it was in 2013. A survey by three Venezuelan universities reckons that 79% of the population are extremely poor and that 30% of under-fives suffer chronic malnutrition or stunting. The dictatorial regime of Nicolás Maduro stays in power by harassing opponents, locking up dissidents and, in some cases, slashing prisoners' feet with razor blades." There appears to be very little hope of a new benevolent leader in Venezuela any time soon.

In the latest Bloomberg news, reporters Patricia Laya and Fabiola Zerpa report that Venezuela has imported 71 tons of bank note security paper to begin printing new Bolivar notes with a value of twenty-three cents. The tragic affect of hyperinflation is driving the Maduro government to take extreme steps to project a façade of control but in reality it wasted precious funds on a foolish measure that benefits no one.

Consider the moving story of a group of strangers who worked together to pull a drowning baby out of a flood, or one about those who removed a vehicle from atop an injured passenger. Someone was directing those emergency rescue efforts from a situational leadership role, a role that was rapidly acquired— and very temporary. Jamie Hernandez, a retired firefighter and emergency responder, did just that in April 2017, while headed to a party with a friend. As reported by NBC News, this group of strangers rescued two babies from an overturned vehicle on a flooded Canton, Texas highway. It all seemed to happen in a split second as Hernandez started resuscitation efforts on the infants. They were saved from drowning and transported to the hospital, where they recovered due to the courageous efforts of strangers.[13]

Business leadership is important. Leaders such as Warren Buffet, with his long record of leading the *Berkshire Hathaway* group, and Jaime Dimon, who leads *JP Morgan Chase*, are frequently sought out for their views on the current financial strength and health of America, as well as their prognosis for its future. Both are proven as effective and credible business leaders, without which their firms would not be nearly as successful.

Recognizing that nothing lasts forever and how important continuity is, Dimon announced the promotion of two senior female executives as part of a succession plan when he retires. Buffett has promoted two senior staffers as vice-chairmen of the *Berkshire Hathaway* Board of Directors. This is a crucial part of leadership, ensuring *future* success and promoting the good of the organization.

In a word—legacy.

Leadership in the medical field is also critically important. The *World Health Organization* (*WHO*) leads efforts to eliminate malaria, a mosquito-borne disease that kills millions each year. Dr. Matshidiso Moeti, Regional Director for Africa, announced in 2018 that Algeria and Argentina are now entirely free of the disease, joining 38 other countries and territories that were previously declared malaria-free. Dr. Moeti said, "Algeria has shown the rest of Africa that malaria can be beaten through country leadership, bold action, sound investment, and science. The rest of the continent can learn from this experience."[14] Bill Gates tweeted his joy in hearing this news on his June 8 *Twitter* post. The *Bill and Melinda Gates Foundation* has been instrumental in providing funding, raising awareness about Malaria and has sought simple, inexpensive, and scalable solutions for many years.[15]

The leadership of President Donald Trump in organizing operation "Warp Speed" to facilitate a speedy, safe, and effective vaccine for this pernicious coronavirus was masterful, necessary, and welcome. He called together the leaders of governmental bureaucracy, scientific community and pharmaceutical industry to cut red tape, attack the virus, and develop a safe and viable vaccine. As of December 2020, there are several Covid-19 vaccines being administered to Americans. These vaccines went through Phase 1, 2 or 3 trials and have been approved by the Food and Drug Administration for use. More are in the pipeline and only time will tell exactly how effective and helpful they are.

Non-profit, academic, governmental, and religious organizations need competent leadership. It is important that there is accountability in financial and legal transactions, for ethical development and growth, and to fulfill stake holder and stockholder expectations. There are decisions to be made, products and services to provide, and visions to fulfill. Without leadership, none of these things will happen in an effective way. Where there is little or no leadership, the potential for financial loss, criminal activity, time theft, misuse of assets, and other problems become all too real.

Competent and ethical leadership is vital to maintain the health of our planet, the lives of our people, and the health of all the organizations that work and serve and live on it. Without proper leadership there will be confusion, uncertainty, and chaos. Where great leadership is lacking, empires that have fallen, entire tribes and ethnic communities have been purged, and horrific wars have been fought. Without competent leadership, businesses and organizations crumble, families quarrel and become estranged, and children rebel and lose their way. Churches split, denominations dissolve, and civil society is horribly impacted—all from a lack of truthful and transparent leaders. When moral decay and evil have prevailed, vast resources, historical treasures, and entire civilizations have been lost because of deficient leadership or because there was none at all.

Yes, it's *that* important.

"Everyone is a leader because everyone influences someone."
— John Maxwell

"Leadership looks like 'a lollipop moment!'"
— Drew Dudley

Chapter Three: What Should It Look Like?

What should a leader look like? I've posed this question to get us to look at leaders and leadership from a different perspective. Our concept of what a leader looks like should be more than one person overseeing a large organization. It is more than that person being responsible to a board of directors, a group of shareholders, Wall Street or angel investors, although these are certainly all components of corporate leadership. It is also the person who leads a small Main Street business, or the head of the Chamber of Commerce, or the dairy farmer, or head librarian. It is the head of the household who works hard to provide the basic physical needs for the family while teaching them the character traits of diligence, honesty, decency, civility, and respect for others. Leaders come from every color, gender, ethnicity, and part of societal strata, and represent varied beliefs and philosophies.

Great leaders practice their craft in venues large and small. What we look for are qualities and character traits, skills and talents, that enable them to lead effectively and to change and elevate individual lives for the better. The passion to create future leaders beyond themselves should be in evidence. They should look like people who deal with problems in healthy, effective, and respectful ways. We should see leaders building relationships, partnerships, and even friendships, seeing and developing the potential in people.

In his book, *Influence People Like Jesus,* leadership expert Jay Brinson describes some of the attributes and skills leaders use when they have significant influence. He also shows how leaders deal with failure—their own, and those of others. In his chapter titled "Invest in People who have failed," he shares some excellent advice:

If you want to become a leader of great influence, forgiveness and restoration must become an essential part of your character. You must develop discernment to see a person's potential through the haze of their failures and lift them to greater usefulness and fruitfulness.

Remember, failure need not be fatal, it can in fact, become the foundation for future greatness.[1]

In contrast, Tim Elmore, a Millennial and Gen Z expert, in his article, "Is Everyone A Leader?" explains why his answer is no. In the traditional definition of a leader, as the head of an organization or business, in charge of people and financial results, he does not believe that everyone is a leader, **nor should they be**. Not everyone is gifted with the talents, or even the personality, to be the CEO at the top of an organizational chart. However, if you ask someone to define an area of strength in their life and how they use it to best influence others for a worthy cause—that *is* a calling and it is another, perhaps better way to describe leadership.

After all, influence is one of the foundations of leadership.

Elmore says, "I believe leadership is intended to be about serving others in the area of our giftedness (strength). When we do, we naturally ripple with influence. We don't even have to try to 'lead' others. As we mature, we are to naturally uncover our area of dominion, and influence a sum of people."[2] Maturity and seasoning are part of being a leader, as well. And he recently Tweeted, "Self-esteem comes from knowing who you are intrinsically, and using your gifts to contribute to a cause greater than yourself."[3]

Drew Dudley, another leadership expert, author, and sought-after speaker has a revealing perspective. In his popular 2010 TEDx talk, aptly titled "Leading with Lollipops," he shared a very important example of leadership. He started by saying that we sometimes make "leadership" bigger than it is and we treat leadership like it is something we will one day deserve or attain, when in reality it is something that can—and should—happen every day as we serve and interact with others. We need to see leaders and measure leadership results in more than just one or two traditional ways.

The everyday things we do are just as valuable and worthy of celebration as the huge, epic, and grandiose things we hope to achieve one day. Dudley gave the example of one action, on one day, that he was completely unaware of until years later. That singular act changed one life for the better. It gave one person hope, confidence ,and self-respect such that when he learned about it, he said the story "literally redefined" his definition of leadership.[4]

Drew Dudley attended a small school in Sackville, New Brunswick. On his last day there, a young lady came up to him and said, "I remember the first time that I met you." Four years earlier, she was just coming to college and was very unsure, so much so that she burst into tears with her parents and said she could not do it. Her parents convinced her to go to the campus and at least look around, promising if she still felt that way, they would take her home.

They also assured her they loved her no matter what.

She was in line to register for classes and looked around and decided she could not do it, after all. This young lady felt peace, and just as she was going to tell her parents to take her home, she saw Dudley come out of the Student Union Building. He was wearing "the stupidest hat" she had ever seen and was holding a sign for the *Shinerama* charity (to help cystic fibrosis patients). He was also carrying a bucket of lollipops.

He was going down the line handing out lollipops and suddenly stopped in front of her and just stared. "It was creepy," she said. But then he gave a lollipop to the man standing next to her and said, "you need to give this lollipop to the beautiful woman standing next to you." The young man turned beet red and would not even look at her. But he gave her the lollipop by extending his hand. Drew got a severe look on his face and looked at her parents and said to them, "Look at that! First day from home and she is already taking candy from a stranger!" Everyone standing nearby howled with laughter, and she said she knew somehow, in that moment, she should not quit school. She said she "knew she was at home," and it would be okay.

She told Drew she had not talked to him in the entire four years she was at the school, but when she heard he was leaving, she had to tell him "he had been an incredibly important person" in her life. She wished him good luck and told him she was still dating that same guy who gave her the lollipop.

Eighteen months later he received an invitation to their wedding.

The "kicker" is that Drew does not remember the lollipop moment at all. It is incredible that the most transformative moment as a leader, the greatest impact he has had on anyone's life, is something he cannot recall. It was so impactful that four years later, someone he did not know came up and told him he was "an incredibly important person" in her life. So in his TEDx talk he asked the question, "How many of you have a lollipop moment, where someone did something or said something that fundamentally made your life better?"[5]

We *can* have an impact on each other's lives, and we need to share and celebrate those moments. Dudley said, "we celebrate birthdays, where all you have to do is not die for 365 days," and yet, we do not celebrate how we positively impact each other. "We need to redefine leadership as *lollipop moments*, where we value the impact on each other's lives more than money and power and titles and influence."[6] Busy-ness does not count as leadership. He asked, "how many tasks do we accomplish during the workday to the possible detriment of personal relationships that impact each other's lives?"[7]

Leadership is often clothed in high and lofty illusions of authority, influence, wealth, and importance, where mere mortals dare not tread or even aspire to gain access to the levels of the elite. But in fact, ordinary people do extraordinary things every day. We need to recognize and value these individuals and their leadership deeds. I can personally identify with Drew's story, because I had my own recent version of a lollipop moment.

There are some wonderful volunteers who work at the reception desk in the rescue mission where I was employed for almost five years. About two years ago, I received a lovely Christmas card from one of the volunteers who had moved away. She wrote a personal note thanking me for being helpful and kind to her as she learned the duties of the reception desk. She noted some of our short discussions and interactions which apparently had positively impacted her. She signed her name.

I'm embarrassed to say that I did not recognize it.

I have no mental picture of her and no idea who this sweet lady is. The lesson from this experience is not only to "take time to smell the roses," but to learn the names of those roses, as well. Since then, I have tried to be more *intentional* and aware to remember faces and names. This was a much needed wake up call. I was too immersed in "busy-ness" and not enough in the importance of getting to know people and building real relationships. This unknown lady taught me a valuable lesson about humanity and relationship awareness.

And I am the better for it.

Drew Dudley spoke passionately about building relationships and serving one another. But also, I learned an important lesson about this from Dr. Benny, a local pastor and community leader. He retired several years ago and moved back to his beloved Tennessee after serving our local community for many years. Dr. Benny pastored a large church and worked with local leaders to start a community ministry for our at-risk and underserved neighbors. He also helped establish and lead a small, local Bible college, where he served as the Chairman for several years.

After completing the official duties chairing his last board meeting, Dr. Benny spoke, in his closing remarks, of his affection and support for the local church community. He reminded us how the church family and leadership play an important role in the lives of individual members, as well as and the community at large. In times of sorrow, trouble, and pain, we seek comfort and solace from spiritual leaders. Here is the gist of what he said:

> *Television and radio ministries are certainly helpful to those who are homebound or lacking transportation. There are upstanding spiritual leaders and preachers like*

Tony Evans, Charles Stanley and others who speak on radio, TV and social media. However, the radio and television preachers are not going to come to your home or hospital room when you are sick or visit your loved ones, or personally comfort you in times of sorrow and pain. They will not be available to officiate at your wedding or preach your funeral or baptize your children. They will not be physically present for the significant events, to celebrate the joys and help you bear the sorrows. That's why we need each other. The local church community start as friends and becomes the family who will personally pray for you, visit you, care for you and help your family in time of need. They will answer the phone in the middle of the night, take you to the grocery store and doctor appointment and love on you when you are depressed and weary.

Dr. Benny could have offered many gems of wisdom, but he chose to speak about the value and role of the local church above all others. He reminded us about the importance of the community, in this case, the community of faith, to live out 1 Cor 12:26, *"If one member suffers, all suffer together; if one member is honored, all rejoice together."* I had not looked at it from this scriptural perspective.

But I do now.

Even if you are not particularly religious, the local community is still a bulwark in times of trouble. Local news stations have broadcast story after story of motorcycle clubs, civic and sports organizations, and local suppliers and restaurants who all come together to raise money, feed and shelter hungry people, and gather supplies and equipment in the wake of hurricanes and tornados. When a child goes missing, people show up with boats, all-terrain vehicles, and even horses to assist law enforcement with the search. People who have never met each other work shoulder to shoulder to accomplish a task or project. And they may never see each other again, but they came together to meet the urgent need at the critical time.

The story of the community outreach ministry that evolved and developed under the guidance and leadership of Dr. Benny and other community leaders is something rather special. The name changed, the offices moved to a new location over the past couple of years, and even the way they serve looks different now. What makes it so special is that I recently became the director of the community outreach ministry. It is an exciting opportunity, and I'm honored to build relationships and learn how to serve the local community in very practical and useful ways.

The future is full of blessings and goodwill.

Lollipop moments happen every day, and we need to appreciate these leaders and shine a light on their examples. One of my Economics professors was very helpful at a time when I was exhausted and discouraged, overwhelmed with full time employment, and family and childcare obligations. His class was not an easy one, and I did not do well on the first test, earning only a D-plus. That was heartbreaking in my first upper-level class. I was quite embarrassed and wanted to quit right there. But I set aside my pride and went to see the professor to see if there was any hope of passing the class.

The professor was kind and he listened to me, that alone was a great encouragement. He saw the desperation on my face and went over the examination question by question. His next words were a comfort, "I see some areas of strong potential here." Those eight words were huge. It was his "lollipop moment" for me, and he never knew how much it helped me. He sounded credible, and I believed him. Two years later I graduated with my degree in Business Economics. Those eight believable and kind words in that "lollipop moment" were a game changer for me. I plan to send a note to the professor to thank him for his kindness and encouragement.

A great leader sometimes leads just one person at a time. The thing is, we never know how our interaction with just one person is going to affect our block, our neighborhood, the larger community, or the entire world. Muhammed Yunus was born in the village of Bathua, by the Kaptai road in Hathazari, Chittagong—in what is now Bangladesh. After securing his degree in economics, he returned to the same poverty-stricken area—to the village of Jobra near Chittagong University. He saw an extreme level of poverty, desperation, and despair in the community.

Dr. Yunus surveyed some of the poorest people in the village and discovered that female basket weavers there were skilled and had potential, but could not borrow money easily. He used $27 of his own money to make "microloans" to forty-two women in 1974, with the average loan amounting to a mere sixty-two cents. They repaid the money quickly, establishing a positive credit record, and from this was born the model for *Grameen Bank*, which has grown to providing millions of microloans. As of 2006, it had 2,211 branches in 70,370 villages serving 6.5 million people and helping to lift them out of abject poverty.[8] This great work started when one man built just 42 relationships, interacting with one at a time, and using $27 of his own meager funds.

In 2018, *Grameen Bank* had more than 20,000 employees and $125 billion in assets. There have been media reports of difficulties and turmoil, where Dr. Yunus' reputation and integrity were questioned by various Bangladeshi leaders. The *Grameen Bank* has been taken over by the government of Bangladesh. He was dismissed from the leadership of the bank, but is still considered by many to be an upstanding individual with valuable contributions to make in the area of finance, politics, and society.[9]

Dr. Yunus is an active speaker and influencer. He was the keynote speaker at the SAP Ariba Live Conference in Singapore in August 2019, as well as at the Italy Capri Summit in that October. He also addressed the United Nations General Assembly regarding Modern Day Slavery and Youth issues in September 2019. The microloan model is currently used to great advantage to help millions of impoverished people improve their circumstances. It is a clever and viable model that has positively impacted the lives of many millions.

The Ripple Effect

"I alone cannot change the world, but I can cast a stone across the waters to create many ripples." This is a quote from Mother Teresa, and it describes another facet of leadership. Our words and deeds affect people with whom we do not have a personal relationship. Our Congressional representatives propose and pass laws that affect millions of Americans. We do not know most of them, but we vote for them. If we have met, it is usually a quick handshake at a town hall meeting or campaign event. There is always some debate as to whether or not our elected officials carry out the will of their constituents or whether they do what *they deem best* for their constituents, even if it is not what they were elected to do, or if they did not read the bill until it was passed.

Their actions impact us—deeply and permanently.

When you throw a pebble into a pond, there is a ripple effect. It may be a tiny little wavelet, but it reaches outward for a great distance. Leadership has ripple effects like this, where the actions of one affect many. Leadership is practiced by individuals, sometimes nefarious, such as dictators, who selfishly serve themselves, e.g., Hitler and Napoleon. Others have humble servant hearts, such as Mother Teresa or Eleanor Roosevelt, and seek to better society for all.

There is a servant-leader in our community—quiet, humble, and effective—where the ripple effect of his influence impacted my life several times. He has been the pastor of the same church for many years. His influence with me is quite impressive, given that I have never met him or attended a service at his church. I'm sure I will meet him some day, but in the meantime, I am still benefitting from the ripple effect of his leadership. I have heard many stories through the years from others who have been positively impacted his leadership, as well. The church he leads has deep roots in the community. Many young lives have been molded by the character and influence of this pastor and his church leadership team.

One young man who was in the youth group there, grew up and left to lead a similar group at another church. Later he served as pastor of his own church. We see a spiritual ripple effect, intergenerational influence, and a positive social impact on the community. One of my good friends is a product of the second generation of leaders who have been mentored and trained in that church. He is now a lay leader in yet another church and is leading others.

One local leader, serving and leading very well, dedicated to his calling, has helped to create another generation of community leaders who also serve and lead well. Those in our community may hazard a guess to his identity, but I will not name him. The focus should instead be on the remarkable example of the ripple effect that positively impacted so many people over so many years, even the people he has never met.

"The function of leadership is to produce more leaders, not more followers."
— Ralph Nader

"I drop kindness pebbles in still water every day, and I watch the effect they have on other people's lives. My favorite kindness pebbles are compliments. Drop a compliment and watch the ripple effect that it has in your life."
— John A. Passaro, Wrestler

"Well sir, we been doing what he has been saying and we are still alive."
— *Unknown soldier, Normandy, 1945*

"Effective leaders are made, not born. They learn from trial and error, and from experience."
— *General Colin Powell*

Chapter Four: Are Leaders Made or Born?

For years, many have expressed strong opinions and given their answers to the formidable question, "Are leaders made or born?" Vince Lombardi, the legendary coach of the Green Bay Packers, and for whom the Super Bowl Trophy is named, said, "Leaders are made, they are not born. They are made by hard effort, which is the price which all of us must pay to achieve any goal that is worthwhile." Leadership expert, Warren Bennis, has been quoted many times saying, "The most dangerous leadership myth is that leaders are born—that there is a genetic factor to leadership. This myth asserts that people simply either have certain charismatic qualities or not. That's nonsense; in fact, the opposite is true. Leaders are made rather than born."

Sort of a chicken and the egg kind of thing—which came first?

I believe the answer to the leadership question is a combination of both. There are some who are thrust into instant leadership in times of war, crisis, or an emergency. Others study, work, train, and develop in a carefully orchestrated trajectory toward a particular leadership position. Still others are naturally charismatic and attract followers like flies to honey. Potential leaders are sometimes born into family business empires or charitable foundations where sons and daughters are expected to one day take up the reins of leadership. None of these scenarios guarantee successful leadership, only that opportunity is sought or presented to the fortunate—or unfortunate—individual.

We have heard about the proverbial "black sheep of the family," where someone either squanders potential and opportunity or just doesn't have what it takes; either way it is a big disappointment. The ne're-do-well just does not live up to the high expectations of the family. Remember Prince Harry and the alleged nude strip billiard game during his wild adventure when he visited "Sin City" Nevada in 2012? The Queen had a few sleepless nights worrying about Harry, but he has since more than redeemed himself.[1] It took some work, growth, and a measure of maturity, but his reputation is better now. He is a family man, husband, father, and global influencer for good causes. He is proof that we can recover from bad choices, even stupid behavior, and learn from our mistakes.

Professors Barry Z. Posner and James Kouzes from Santa Clara University are very strong in their belief that leadership can be taught—people can learn how to be leaders. To them, the idea that "leadership is magical, ethereal, esoteric, or reserved for only a very few" is just shy of ridiculous. "It is just pure myth that only a lucky few can ever understand the intricacies of leadership. Leadership is not a gene, and it's not a secret code that can't be deciphered by ordinary people." They go on to say that leadership involves "an observable set of skills and abilities" no matter who is leading or where they are doing so."[2]

They argue that "any skill can be developed, strengthened, and enhanced given enough motivation, along with practice and feedback, role models, and coaching."[3] Leadership is much more than a set of inherent personality traits. It takes hard work, perseverance, and sacrifice. These are qualities and attributes that most anyone can develop and use without involving luck, magic, or even myth.

Leadership can also be loud, messy and occasionally brutal, as we will see in the following story of Sargeant Dougherty.

Are Leaders Made?

A while back, I mentioned my father-in-law. Joseph H. Dougherty was a veteran of World War II and was one of thousands who stormed the beaches at Normandy on D-Day on June 6, 1944. He was a humble farm boy from southwest Virginia who served with 29th Infantry Division, 116th Regiment, 3rd Battalion, M Company. That entire division saw horrific losses, particularly in the early moments of the battle. In fact, the famous "Bedford Boys" were in the 29th. Twenty-two soldiers from tiny Bedford, Virginia (pop. 3,200) died that day—19 of them in the first moments of the battle. Their sacrifice is honored by the fact that the National D-Day Memorial is located in Bedford.

My father-in-law's company arrived at Omaha Beach in a specially outfitted landing craft. As they disembarked in shallow water, they immediately took enemy fire, then drifted to shore by hiding among floating corpses of already dead soldiers. Upon reaching dry ground, they fought their way to the top of first hill, where Joe found three bullet holes in his field jacket. His gas mask had also been shot through, but he was unharmed.

The 116th suffered 1,007 casualties on D-Day.

In the chaos that followed, Allied troops pushed forward. The fighting was fierce. They were trying to take a forward position away from the Germans, but there were German troops *behind* them, as well. PFC Dougherty came upon a fellow soldier lying on the ground in a fetal position, terrified and trembling with fear. He tried to get the soldier to move, but he wouldn't budge. In desperation, Dougherty started kicking the man in the rear and yelling at him, "Do you want to die right here? Do you think you are going to live forever? Get up!" The soldier dug deep, found his courage, got to his feet, and stumbled forward.

PFC Dougherty and his unit were ambushed and pinned down somewhere between the beach landing and the town of Saint-Lo. During the ambush, both the Sargent and Corporal of the squad were killed. With no chain of command, the soldiers panic set in. PFC Dougherty, a machine gunner, realized if they stayed in their current position, they would all die right there. He saw some woods behind them and thought if they could make it to the tree cover they would have a better chance of survival. He shouted for the squad to retreat to the woods, telling them that he would give them cover fire, then they could cover him once they made it to the woods. He recalled that he just, "opened up with the machine gun" yelling to the men, "Go! Go! Go!" They followed his orders, and everyone made it safely to the woods.

Over the next few days, the hungry, scared, and exhausted group of soldiers banded together. They eventually stumbled upon another group led by an Army Captain—they never knew his name. The Captain asked where their Sargent and Corporal were and was advised that both were dead. The Captain then asked who was leading them. One of the soldiers pointed at PFC Dougherty and said, "Well sir, we've been doing what he's been saying and we're still alive." The Captain gave PFC Dougherty a battlefield promotion right then and there. He became Sergeant Dougherty, and he held that rank until he was honorably discharged several years later.

After the war, and throughout his life, almost everyone called my father-in-law, Joe. He will tell you he was not trying to be a leader, but just trying to stay alive and keep everyone else alive. However, something in him rose up, a confidence that was almost visible and tangible, so that the men looked to their new Sergeant for structure, strategy, and even comfort. They gave him their respect and loyalty, and he did his best to serve them during a time of great peril and hardship.

Throughout his life, Joe served as a leader in his community, political party, and in the school system where he was employed. My father-in-law was a man of strong opinions. So am I. And we disagreed on many occasions. He was not without fault or flaw. But, in a time of crisis or danger, I would put my life in his hands, gladly.

Sergeant Dougherty was elevated to a position of leadership that day on the battlefield. He was an authentic hero, having earned a Purple Heart and other awards for service and valor. Joe always tried to encourage others to rise up and not stay in stagnant state. To stay alert and cultivate friends and acquaintances, he returned to college in his sixties, in part, to keep his life lively and interesting. Joe never met a stranger and could have a rousing conversation with almost anyone. His brother Ralph said he could make friends with a doorknob!

Did my father-in-law have innate leadership skills or were they acquired when he went through basic training? What if he had skills and character traits that had been nurtured in him as he grew up and these were burnished in basic training and maybe he acquired even more expertise during boot camp? It would certainly make a strong argument for the notion that a leader could be born *and* made.

Psychologist Tim Elmore has an interesting observation about how leaders develop and lead. He cautions against forcing anyone to lead if they are not a natural "take charge" type person. He advocates, especially for mentors, to help emerging leaders find their area of strength and gifting. Then they will follow their passion and find their area of leadership.

He believes there are two kinds of leaders: *habitual* leaders and *situational* leaders. The habitual leaders feel good about taking charge. It is easy and natural for them to do so. They gravitate toward leadership and are not at all uncomfortable being in charge. They are also used to taking charge as a practical habit.[4]

Other leaders, those from the rest of the population, are not natural or habitual leaders. When the situation arises where their gifting and strength is engaged, they "come alive and become the right one to lead in that particular situation." It is a time where they shine and feel their sense of purpose being fulfilled.[5]

There is a deeper theory of situational leadership, the *Hersey-Blanchard Situational Leadership Theory*, named after its developers, Dr. Paul Hersey, author of *The Situational Leader*, and Kenneth Blanchard, author of *One-Minute Manager*.

This method involves identifying and using the correct leadership style, given the maturity level of those being led. The primary foundation of situational leadership is flexibility, which plays a large part in successful leadership. There is not really a "best" style of leadership, according to Hershey and Blanchard. The goal is to be effective and get the job done. Therefore, the most successful leaders are those who can assess the willingness and skill set of their followers. The leader will then adapt to that group based on their skills and level of maturity, as well as the task to be completed.[6]

Are Leaders Born?

Prince Charles, Prince William, and Prince Harry of Great Britain (regarded at one time as the black sheep prince) are close heirs to the throne. Born into their roles, they have been groomed and schooled since birth to prepare to ascend one day. They literally have royal blood flowing through their veins. Is their genetic makeup so different than British rock star and former Beatle, Ringo Starr, who came from rather humble beginnings in the same country? Or did the advantage of economic and educational opportunities, combined with tutoring, royal training, and monarchial role models enable the Princes to be nurtured and prepared for the role as a king, instead of the role of successful international rock star (a different kind of "royalty")?

Sir Richard Starkey, better known as Ringo Starr, has been a Member of the British Empire, MBE for twenty-five years, and is the recent recipient of another distinguished honor. In 2018, he was appointed a Knight Commander of the Order of the British Empire by Prince William, second heir in line to the British throne. A media photograph of the Prince shows him attired in full official royal regalia, complete with a sword, which he used to perform the formal knighting ceremony for Starkey (Ringo) at Buckingham Palace.[7] Not bad for a poor boy from Liverpool whose skill set is most represented used on the surface of a Ludwig drum set—or in his songs.

Raised in a very poor family in Dingle, Liverpool, Ringo suffered from multiple childhood illnesses, and his start at drumming was tapping on a cabinet beside his bed while being treated for tuberculosis. Needless to say, he did not fare well in school due to extended illness and absence. But when he got a second-hand drum set given from his stepfather as a Christmas gift in 1957, he never looked back. Ringo Starr lead the way for innovation and creativity in the use of percussive instruments. He became a legend in his own time.

Ringo is one of the most famous drummers of all time. He has been imitated by thousands. In *Classic Rock Drummers*, it says, "Ringo's fat tom sounds and delicate cymbal work were imitated by thousands of drummers."[8] On the website of the *Percussive Arts Society*, contributor Robyn Flats wrote: "I cannot count the number of drummers who have told me that Ringo inspired their passion for drums."

He used his influence to engage more drummers to use modern techniques, such as the matched grip, which is achieved by "tuning the drums lower, and using muffling devices on tonal rings."[9]

Who knew?

President John F. Kennedy and both Presidents Bush were raised in families with long histories of public service. These large and influential families participated in politics in significant ways that influenced American history, forming rich family legacies. They were raised with economic and academic advantages and then taught and nurtured in an environment where leadership was expected and desired. Was their genetic make-up a significant factor, and did it contribute to their ability to lead and to their prospects of pursuing leadership roles? Others in their families, Robert and Ted Kennedy, Jeb Bush, and their children, were also very prominent in political activities. Does this lend any credence to the idea that leaders are born and possess some mythical leadership gene, instead of being developed through nurturing, learning, and following the example of other leaders?

Dr. Elliott Jaques was a gifted clinic psychologist and medical doctor with degrees from Harvard and John Hopkins Universities. He believed an "individual's cognitive capacity, which is roughly equivalent to IQ, is set at birth." Jaques argued that an individual's leadership ability "is inherently tied to cognitive capacity." This being said, he believed there was no reason to engage in any type of leadership training because the amount and quality of capability and potential was already set and could not be increased.[10]

Thomas Carlyle, a Scottish philosopher and author, published lectures back in 1840 on his "Great Man Theory." He posited that the choices, attributes, and ideas of great men, heroes if you will, have greatly contributed to our progress and to important historical events. Throughout his series of lectures, *On Heroes, Hero-worship*, and the *Heroic in History*, he used the words "intrinsic" and "intrinsically." Carlyle believed great leaders were born and ready for service when called upon by events.[11] Webster's Dictionary defines intrinsic as "belonging to the essential nature or constitution of a thing," and lists synonyms such as "built-in" or "hard-wired."[12]

Contemporary philosopher, sociologist and anthropologist, Herbert Spencer, fiercely disagreed with Carlyle. He believed those so called "great men" were simply benefiting from their environment, education, and nurturing. This sounds somewhat like the Bush and Kennedy families. Spencer wrote in his book, *The Study of Sociology*:

> *But if all biological science, enforcing all popular belief, convinces you that by no possibility will an Aristotle come from a father and mother with facial angles of fifty degrees, and that out of a tribe of cannibals...there is not the remotest chance of a Beethoven arising; then you must admit that the genesis of the great man depends on the long series of complex influences which has produced the*

race in which he appears, and the social state into which that race has slowly grown. If it be a fact that the great man may modify his nation in its structure and actions, it is also a fact that there must have been those antecedent modifications constituting national progress before he could be evolved. Before he can re-make his society, his society must make him. So that all those changes of which he is the proximate initiator have their chief causes in the generations he descended from. If there is to be anything like a real explanation of these changes, it must be sought in that aggregate of conditions out of which both he and they have arisen.[13]

The question of "nature vs. nurture" will continue to be debated and examined. Is it true that great leaders are endowed at birth with the traits and abilities they need to rise to the occasion? Or does great instruction from mature and knowledgeable individuals already in leadership produce future great leaders? A debate was conducted by two groups from the Academic Leadership Fellows Program at the *American Association of Colleges of Pharmacy* (AACP) Interim Meeting in Tampa, Florida in February 2016. A good deal of time and effort was invested in studying, researching, and debating this very question.

Those on opposing sides examined the question of whether leaders are made or born. Both groups presented solid arguments and evidence and thoroughly examined both nature (genetic/component) and nurture (environment/ influence). The group supporting the position that leaders are born examined the heredity of leadership in the study of fraternal twins Scott and Mark Kelly, two Naval and NASA officers (astronauts). The twins are well known for leading teams and conducting research in space. One group examining their research determined a genetic component indicated great potential for leadership, but to fulfill that role also required a fostering and nurturing environment. There was not a great deal empirical evidence available about the genetic component, but there was much more to support the *combination* of nature and nurture.

The same group also examined research conducted on pairs of fish, where one fish had shown leadership and the other follower tendencies. The studies tested small rewards of food to follower fish when they displayed leadership tendencies, but did not reward the leader fish for leading. The result was that the pairs of fish received less food when the followers were nudged toward leadership. The study concluded that while fish could be taught to follow, it was hard for a follower to *learn* to lead. If this study is extended to human research, the results could be similar.

The counterpoint group examined attributes that can be learned and developed, such as integrity, the ability to inspire, passion for hope and optimism, curiosity, and risk taking. They looked at the failures of Walt Disney before he succeeded, as well as those of John Rockefeller, Sr., Dwight D. Eisenhower, and others who did not initially come from a favored or privileged background. They concluded that leadership traits can be learned and developed, buttressed by the fact that U.S. corporations spend over 14 billion dollars each year on the training and development of leaders.

The study took place over several months, with several meetings, mock debates, and preparation. Their conclusion was: "Historical examples exist to support both a genetic and environmental component to leadership....Leaders most likely come from a combination of genetic predisposition and development through reactions to environmental factors."[14]

Why Do We Need development?

One of the most intriguing answers to the "born or made" question may be found in a simple *Google* search. When the search phrase "leadership development," is more than ***one billion options*** are available for examination. Distilling these down to a more manageable number by searching for "*executive* leadership development," the yield is ***260 million results***. This begs the question to proponents of the "leaders are born not made" school of thought: If leaders are born and not made, why are there so many programs, articles, courses, seminars, books, instructors, and advertisements for leadership development—and why is so much money spent on it?

Harvard Business Review reports, "Leadership development represents a huge and growing investment for most organizations. Industry research, for example, shows that companies spent more than $24 billion on leadership and management training worldwide in 2013, an increase of 15% from 2012."[15] Even if leaders are born, they need to learn, develop, and refine their traits. Thus, the need for leadership development is growing and robust. Many executives, politicians and other leaders avail themselves of these resources.

And yet, the question remains, "Are leaders made or born?"

"Self-leadership is the influence we exercise over ourselves to establish the motivation and direction we need to be effective in life and at work. Also, self-leadership can create a foundation for our performance without having to rely and depend on others."
— *Charles Manz*

"Personal leadership is not a singular experience. It is, rather, the ongoing process of keeping your vision and values before you and aligning your life to be congruent with those most important things."
– *Steven Covey*

Chapter Five: Knowing and Leading Yourself

Throughout history, leaders have been conduits for new ideas and at the forefront of societal changes in society, government, religion, and culture. Leaders influence and motivate others to embrace an idea or philosophy and then commit their time and resources toward a common purpose. Adolf Hitler and Martin Luther King Jr. were both wildly popular and charismatic leaders who influenced and led millions of people to take extraordinary actions. But only one of them was a change agent for the good of society and humanity, while the other sought to exterminate an entire race and all vestiges of their identity. Followers, whether the leader is good or evil, tend to take on the persona of the individual in the lead position.

The results of leadership depend upon the moral code, character attributes, beliefs, skill, and influence of the leader. Over time, the way we individually handle our emotions, the way we choose our reactions, the tone of voice, body language and demeanor, the words we speak or don't speak, or the timing of speaking, all determine how effective our leadership will be. There are many words of wisdom already written to guide us in the decisions we make and how we choose to conduct ourselves as individuals who might chose to be leaders.

From the ancient sanctuary Temple of Apollo at Delphi, to the Apostle Paul, to the Jedi Knight Warrior of *Star Wars* fame, Yogini Yoda, many notable messengers have encouraged humans to "Know thyself." This maxim has been used for centuries to motivate and encourage humanity to seek deep awareness, understanding, and knowledge about one's self. There are abundant and pertinent reasons to do so, but in the pursuit of leadership, it is imperative to first know and lead yourself well. Only then can you begin to understand how to lead others well and earn the respect and credibility necessary to inspire individuals to cooperate and perform with efficiency and excellence.

I'm a *Star Wars* fan who enjoys the quintessential battle between good (The Resistance) and evil (the dark side), in a galactic setting far, far away. The saga has themes and lessons on life, love, and leadership. My favorite character is the Jedi

Knight, Yogini Yoda, who trains Jedi Knight candidates while speaking Pennsylvania Dutch-esque words of wisdom. To be selected as a candidate for Jedi training was a great honor. The training involved hardship, sacrifice, and rigorous mental and physical conditioning in dangerous and remote locations.

One of the main characters, Luke Skywalker, was a young X-wing fighter pilot, and a naturally gifted Jedi candidate. He was also cocky, distracted, and uncommitted. With the fate of the entire universe at stake, Yoda was not going to waste precious time on any candidate who was not entirely serious and committed to the training process. In *The Empire Strikes Back*, Yoda reflects on the attitude of Luke, "A Jedi must have the deepest commitment, the most serious mind. This one a long time have I watched. All his life has he looked away…to the future, to the horizon. Never his mind on where he was. Hmm? What he was doing."[1]

Over time, Luke became a respected leader in the Resistance but only after he trained and practiced honing his skills. He also studied and reflected on his life to discover who he was and what he was willing to sacrifice. Yoda required a commitment of all mental, spiritual, and physical abilities. In *Return of the Jedi*, he admonished Luke against the powerful allure of evil and counselled him to have patience, conquer his fears, and live by a high moral code. "Anger, fear, aggression.

The dark side are they. Once you start down the dark path forever will it dominate your destiny."[2]

Luke's father, a former Jedi Warrior, is now known—Darth Vader, an evil leader who was lured away by the power of the dark side. He desperately wanted Luke to join him and tempted him to come to the dark side. He appealed to his son's deep emotions and anger during a light saber duel. Luke would have great power and position by joining his father to rule and reign as Imperial leaders.

The young Jedi resisted, fumbled in the fighting and lost the light saber duel when Vader sliced off one of his hands. Wounded and weakened, Luke decided to jump to his death instead of joining the dark side. He was rescued by fellow warriors, while precariously dangling at the bottom of a space trash chute. As he recovered, he was humble, wise and began his way toward maturity to develop into the strong, inspiring leader Yoda knew he could become. Before he could be an example to lead others, he had to learn who he was, what he believed, and mold and solidify his moral code, as well as his commitment to the cause.

Much has been written about the struggle between good and evil, the pursuit of excellent character, and the importance of knowing and improving ourselves, through the tools of self-examination, reflection and correction. Some writings, like the *Star Wars* movie saga, are fictional, but nevertheless teach us to adopt a high personal moral code and practice wisdom, kindness, perseverance, and humility.

Personal stories are also great teaching tools. One noteworthy example is Zig Ziglar, a Christian leader, successful salesman, author, and motivational speaker. He was called America's Merchant of Hope by the *Texas Monthly* magazine. Mr. Ziglar had a lot of wisdom and is quoted frequently. About knowing yourself he said, "Most people have a picture of themselves that is so narrow and so shallow it bears no resemblance to who they are and what they can do. Most people have no idea what they can do, because all they've been told is what they can NOT do. Most people don't know what they can do because they don't know who they are."[3]

The Holy Bible, written by forty inspired authors, over a period of 2,000 years, contains accurate historical writings about many people, places, and events. There are lessons about how to choose our words, our reactions, our decisions, and how to live our lives. The book of Proverbs is chock full of practical guidance about things to avoid and what we should and should not do and say and think. We ideally should choose humility, goodness, wisdom, and other desirable and noble qualities.

In the New Testament Book of Matthew, we find in Chapter seven a parable where Jesus uses the metaphor of the speck and the beam in regard to judging others. He admonishes us to first conduct self-examination and self-improvement before critiquing others. The person with the beam in their own eye need not examine their neighbor to discover and judge his small flaws until they have identified and corrected their own many faults.

In the Old Testament book of Lamentations 3:40-41, we are encouraged by the Prophet Jeremiah to "search out and examine our ways and turn back to the Lord; Let us lift our hearts and hands to God in heaven." We are advised to perform an internal self-examination then work to correct our faults. In the New Testament, 2 Corinthians 13:5 the Apostle Paul exhorts us in the same vein to "Examine yourselves, whether ye be in the faith, prove your own selves. Know ye not your own selves, how that Jesus Christ is in you, except ye be reprobates?"

We are also encouraged in various other books of the Bible, such as Acts 20:28, "Pay careful attention to yourselves…." And 1 Timothy 4:16, "Keep a close watch on yourself…" It seems to be the individual responsibility of each person to keep a watch over themselves.

Why Is It Important to Know Myself?

One of the primary reasons to know yourself is so you can be aware of who you are and what you want to accomplish in life. Then, and only then, can you determine how to get there. It is also quite helpful in forming and developing our personal and professional relationships. For example, there are individuals who decide they want to work very hard for a specified time period and then retire early. Others want a dozen children or, no children at all, and want to travel the world. Knowing who you are, what you want, and how you will get there will help to communicate your goals and intentions to a potential employer, business partner, or even your spouse.

When the relationship starts to spark and hum you should take the time to clearly communicate your intentions, especially when there could be a significant lifestyle change. Working extra nights and weekends to enhance your financial or vocational situation may prevent you from assisting your partner in childcare, changing diapers, doing laundry and dishes, and other domestic tasks. The tug-of-war between employment and marriage and family will cause undue suffering unless each party buys in.

Your dream job can become a nightmare and your loving spouse can grow angry and bitter because you did not clearly communicate your intentions. Having a likeminded partner in life is necessary to assure they are willing to participate. You should have mutual goals and aspirations, or it simply will not work.

When it comes to being an effective leader, it is critically important to know yourself in all the good, bad, and ugly of your makeup. T. J. Addington, writing about leadership and emotional health, says, "The best leaders and the healthiest individuals are those who know their own vulnerabilities, dark sides, and lack of knowledge. The truth is that we know very little, are often wrong, often misjudge others, and have dark sides that are far worse than we want to believe. Personal health comes from knowing the truth about ourselves, not from lying to ourselves. How we see ourselves will impact how we see and treat others and their views."[4] The way we treat others and their views is directly related to how they regard us as leaders.

We also need to know and understand ourselves to better regulate how we deal with situations that cause anxiety. Leaders who react badly to anxiety will tend to instill fear and alienate followers. They do not have the requisite tools or disposition to be steady leaders. Addington writes, "How we learn (and it is learned) to handle that anxiety is one of the key factors in how well we will lead over the long haul. Those who don't handle anxiety well will sabotage their leadership either through emotional responses that are inappropriate or through inner turmoil that eats at their gut - and often both."[5]

Counting the Opportunity costs

In the discipline of Economics, the subject of "opportunity costs" is a frequent item of discussion, producing many interesting examples. An opportunity cost is what you forgo to pursue another activity or opportunity. It may be the choice of buying a new car or saving for that once-in-a-lifetime trip to Paris. It is the cost, tangible or intangible, in time, money, sacrifice, or effort, using a resource to do or acquire one thing and not do or acquire another thing.

If you commit to work for an organization, the opportunity cost for you is at least forty hours per week of your time committed to that job and employer. You give up the right to do something else with those forty hours because you are being paid to use it for the benefit of the organization and not for your own pursuits or interests. And when you work, whether during the day, night, or on weekends, is usually the choice of the employer—not yours. They often choose premium daylight and weekend hours as their claim on your time.

I know a young man with a wonderful wife, two handsome sons, and a good job. He works as a service technician, is paid a nice hourly rate, and drives a company vehicle. He has voiced the desire that he would like to become an entrepreneur and have his own business. Before he makes that move, he needs to develop a solid business plan, after investigating the best type of business to pursue. He will need to consider his skills, the demand for them, what he is capable and willing to do, and how much he can charge for his services or products. In concert with that information and plan, he will need to build a cash reserve to launch the business and keep his family in beans and socks for a while.

As a potential entrepreneur, he should first ask himself some very serious questions, such as how hard is he willing to work? Will he work very long hours for a season to start the business and move it to being profitable? Will he be the family *and* business leader, and the only employee, for a while? Is he willing to give up family and leisure time, hobbies, and extras to make it a success? There is a new baby in the house. Is he willing to take risks with savings to invest in his new business, commit to nights, weekends, holidays, no vacations, and have very little spare change? And most important, does this goal have the mutual consent of his wife? After all, she has a large stake of time, effort, and sacrifice in this endeavor, also.

In Luke Chapter 14, Jesus asked the disciples if it was wise to count the cost of building a tower to make sure you have enough money to complete the project? This easily translates into a lesson on counting the cost of any noble pursuit, including opening a new business or taking the lead of an existing organization. Are you willing to take risks, be responsible, and pay the price to be a leader? Indeed, what are you willing to do? How hard are you willing to work? And what are you willing to sacrifice to assume the position of "leader"?

How Can I Know Myself?

Peter Drucker, the quintessential leadership expert, said that we live in a time of great opportunity and responsibility. It is possible to manage yourself well and have great advancement, but to do so, "you'll need to cultivate a deep understanding of yourself—not only what your strengths and weaknesses are but also how you learn, how you work with others, what your values are, and where you can make the greatest contribution. Success in the knowledge economy comes to those who know themselves—their strengths, their values, and how they best perform."[6]

In 1972 psychologists Shelley Duval and Robert Wicklund developed and published their theory of self-awareness. They wrote: "When we focus our attention on ourselves, we evaluate and compare our current behavior to our internal standards and values. We become self-conscious as objective evaluators of ourselves." In layman's terms, self-awareness means we can look at our actions and see how they align with our values. We can continuously monitor our thoughts, feelings, aspirations, and needs, using this information to help us refine and improve our internal values and increase our self-esteem—then align our external behavior to match.[7] We have a good idea of how hard we want to work and align our work efforts with our goals. We can also use self-awareness to avoid anxiety by advocating for ourselves to change the outcome of stress inducing situations.

Doing the Hard Work of Change

An example of reducing anxiety is found in the area of becoming more assertive, advocating for a better outcome, position, or benefit for ourselves and others. Lobbying for a raise or promotion is a prime way to advocate for myself. If there is a need to stay late or work on the weekend, the most compliant team members may pull (get stuck with!) this duty more often. To change this outcome, they begin by declining the request and pointing out they or others have already stayed late several times. Next, they politely assert it is time for one who has not stayed late to do so and offer to brief that member on what to expect when working late on the project. Providing information and encouragement helps others take on these tasks and assures them they will not be "stuck." This process helps both the individual undertaking the transformation to being more assertive. It also helps the team by allowing others to view us more positively as we grow in self-confidence.

This kind of assertion reminds the team that each member is to be equally respected, valued, and is deserving of equitable time off. This is especially effective where we have taken the time to lead by example and have volunteered to stay late or work over a weekend. By monitoring our internal feelings and knowing when we are entering an uncomfortable area, it helps us to speak up, politely and firmly, to change an outcome. It proactively aids to prevent potential feelings of resentment, and it distributes the positive and negative tasks to other team members fairly. Self-advocacy and polite assertion also help reduce self-guilt and other negative feelings by giving us small successes to celebrate.

However, if you willingly accepted a position with the serious responsibilities, perks and compensation of upper leadership, it is assumed you would accept the attendant inconveniences and difficulties. Before taking on a position with such obligations, you would ask yourself (and your family) if you (and they) are willing to accept the long hours and responsibility. Can they withstand the inconvenience and intrusion on leisure and family time, birthdays, holidays, meals, and sleep time? If you and your family are not willing to do so, then you should be transparent and honest with your employer or potential employer and decline such a promotion or position.

In our professional and personal lives, we should strive to conduct ourselves according to a moral code, a set of internal values that guide and direct our actions and reactions. These values become part of us. Knowing ourselves well means recognizing when we are in danger of violating these values, not living up to our moral code, and placing ourselves in a precarious position. We must guard against becoming overwhelmed, stressed, anxious, or exhausted—and be vigilant to exercise care when we are.

Leading ourselves well means that we are kind even when we are exhausted, and courteous and careful on the road despite our stress level. Our temper is held even at the end of long day and we are in the express check-out lane at the grocery store and "that" person cuts in front of us with 22 items, when the limit is 15. It means practicing self-restraint, courtesy, civility, and being an example to our children, peers, and friends even when we are exhausted or experiencing great stress.

Of course, we will not perform perfectly every time. Failure is a part of life, but it doesn't have to be our identity. We are human and our self-control is mightily tested when we feel overwhelmed and exhausted. We do our best not to let our feelings cloud our behavior or judgment, but when we do. We correct our course, apologize, and make amends. We learn from that experience and resolve to do better—and be better--as individuals and leaders.

T. J. Addington recommends "think time" to help us become better leaders. In his book *Deep Influence* he writes, "Think time needs to be very high on our lists if we want to be people of deep influence."[8] He recommends regularly setting aside time on the calendar to actually schedule appointment s *with ourselves* to help us disconnect from the busy-ness of life, clear our heads, and organize our thoughts. We can unplug, unwind, and take a look at our internal character, values—not to mention, how we regulate our emotions. By considering the answers and looking at the success and failure of the day, we can catch small problems before they turn into big failures.

In each daily transaction and interaction we have the choice of how we respond. During her speech at the 2016 Democratic National Convention, then First Lady Michelle Obama spoke about she and the President sought to manage the effects of life in the White House regarding their two daughters. She said that when people spoke negatively about the President, their motto was, "when they go low, we go high." She was referring to the choice of how to respond to the offending words and deeds of others.[9]

Great advice!

It is difficult to change ingrained negative habits and behaviors that have developed over many years. To begin with, we first must acknowledge them and become acutely aware of how and when they occur. This is not easy—to admit faults or errors—but it is *always* the first step. To promote correction and change in the pursuit of self-improvement it is helpful to enlist the assistance of friends, family, and co-workers.

Whether it is a quest to lose weight, stop interrupting the other person, or conquering procrastination, we should ask with a humble attitude and a sincere desire to change. Most people are happy and willing to help, but be aware—this involves their efforts to hold you *accountable*. If you ask for help, be prepared for honest feedback and receive it without getting defensive. This process fosters better behavior, new habits, and improves our personal and professional relationships by building trust.

Writing for *Fortune* magazine, Peter Gollwitzer, a professor of psychology at *New York University*, has advice for those trying to break bad habits and develop new ones on the way to reaching their goals. There is much research in the field of motivation science which suggests that greater success can be found if we make deliberate plans on how to change our habits and behaviors.[10] Those who are seeking to overcome substance abuse are urged to avoid the people, places, and things that trigger their addictions. Obviously, an alcoholic would seek to avoid his old drinking buddies at their favorite neighborhood watering hole, as well as refraining from purchasing all things alcoholic.

Bad habits in areas such as work, social life, and personal health are the result of stress, anxiety, and/or poor choices. An effective way to begin transformation is to "specify when, where, and how you want to act upon your goals" by using a preset plan called "if-then." *If* I am stressed and find myself reaching for the bag of pretzels, *then* I plan a short walk outside instead. *If* I get into another political argument with my brother-in-law, *then* I will say "okay, we all have our opinions" and seek another conversation in the room. Making a plan is a significant way to achieve a successful outcome, because, over time, it becomes an almost automatic response. Encountering the dilemma initiates the preplanned response and we simply follow the plan, building on initial successes to become more successful until the behavior is transformed.

Working on no more than one or two areas at a time, where we desire change, is optimal. If we try to change every possible thing that may be wrong all at the same time, we will likely become overwhelmed and quit. It is rather like trying to run three miles the first day you decide to work out as part of a New Year's resolution. You will probably not make it more than 300 yards before becoming discouraged and disillusioned. Instead, make a goal for yourself that is attainable, such as brisk walking 30 minutes a day for a week. Build on small and consistent successes and keep moving your goal forward.

Persistence and perseverance are keys to success with any goal.

And they are an important part of leadership.

"He (Billy Graham) had a deep impact on my life as a principled colleague and spiritual mentor, who taught me that the life one leads is more important than the mere words one says."
— *A. Larry Ross*

"A leader with a fistful of credibility can surmount almost any obstacle. Without credibility, most of his or her influence will vanish like snow on a warm spring day."
— *J. David Newman*

Chapter Six: Leadership Credibility

Credibility is a critical part of leadership. So vital, that we should spend a great deal of time thinking about it, studying it, keeping it safe, learning how to repair it if it is strained, and actively work every day to avoid it being damaged. Influence is one of our most powerful tools in leadership—but it only works if we are credible. Much of the job of a leader is to persuade. Persuasion is emotional in nature. We sway opinions, change people's minds, cajole, encourage, and nudge our followers. We ask them to work harder, set aside differences and work as a team, adopt core beliefs and common goals, and we set an example for them to follow.

When I was a child, both of my parents were heavy smokers, but they constantly told my sister, brother, and me not to smoke. They said, "do as I say, not as I do." *Hmmm*, that didn't work very well then, and it doesn't work any better now. Mom and Dad both lacked credibility in the "no smoking" department. My siblings and I all smoked at some point in our lives—some longer than others. None of us smoke now, but it was a hard battle for me to quit, and I know it was not a walk in the park for my siblings.

My parents, however, did teach us many wonderful things such as the value of hard work, helping others in need, being generous, and why it is so important to empower people to help themselves. Giving someone a handout is only temporary, and it can rob a person of their dignity. Along with a life-long belief in God, we also learned to be self-sufficient, always have a back-up plan, and other helpful life-lessons. Something else they taught was very important, I learned was that it was easier to be honest than to remember a lie, and then tell another one to cover it up. Dad always said that if I messed up, to tell him upfront. The punishment, if merited, would be much less than if he found out about it from someone else. That was true then, and it is true now.

I mentioned a quote from Barry Z. Posner, professor of leadership at Santa Clara University, in an earlier chapter. He and colleague, Jim Kouzes, wrote a book about *Leadership Credibility* in 1994, and it remains extremely relevant more than 25 years later. In fact, it is a required text in some premier institutions where courses on Organizational Leadership are taught. They write about the importance of earning and retaining the trust and confidence of your followers. While some of their students were from the business realm, the lessons they taught are universal for all who would lead or aspire to lead in any arena.

They asked a simple, but pointed question, "Why would someone follow you?" During thirty years of interviews, surveys, and research, they distilled the list of the most important and necessary leadership traits down to just these four: *competency*, *honesty*, *forward-thinking*, and *being inspirational*. Their premise was straightforward: people will respond to and trust those who are *credible*. Examples abound of leaders having one, two, or even three of these traits in force, but their leadership credibility still had gaps and wrinkles. This, in turn, strained their relationships with their followers. It is helpful to examine a few examples to see just how expensive (literally and figuratively) and how impactful the loss of credibility can be.

Tiger Woods: Ten Years to Recovery

Tiger Woods was the number one professional golfer in the world in 2009, and at the time he led a very quiet, low profile life. He was a role model to many young golfers and young people in general. Tiger inspired minority students toward excellence in scholastic achievement. His wife was a beautiful ex-model, his children were healthy and well behaved, and he was a famous sports icon. He was a sought-after speaker, influencer, and role model. He was well paid by premier sponsors for endorsements ($100 million in his top earning year) such as *Gillette*, *Accenture*, *AT&T*, *General Motors*, and *Gatorade*. Many of these firms later dropped him from their roster of endorsers when, in the Winter of 2009, a salacious sex scandal went public.

Tiger earned millions as a golfer, with various estimates of his net worth ranging from $50-$75 million dollars. Investors and firms had high confidence in him as a trustworthy professional and credible role model, worthy of endorsing their products and services. Fans viewed Tiger in the golf hat and shirt bearing the logo swoosh of *Nike*. He promoted other corporate logos, particularly the premier *Rolex Oyster Perpetual* wristwatch. He lost his credibility when it was revealed he had committed adultery with multiple women, including the rumors he had frequent sexual encounters with porn stars, as well. This damaged the well cultivated image of being a wholesome, measured, mature, and responsible individual who was known for "having it all together."

His personal net worth and earnings were decimated by the loss of sponsors and a costly divorce settlement. His immoral and offensive behavior also affected stockholders in the various firms that paid him for his endorsements, companies such as *Proctor and Gamble*, who own *Gillette* brand razors, *PepsiCo*, owner of the *Gatorade* brand, *Nike*, and *Conde Nast*, the publisher of *Golf Digest* magazine. A study by two professors of Economics at the *University of California at Davis*, Christopher Knittel and Victor Stango, revealed that "stock market returns for the 13 trading days that fell between Nov. 27, the date of the car crash that ignited the Woods' scandal, and Dec. 17, a week after the golf great announced his indefinite leave from the sport and the scandal reduced shareholder value in the sponsor companies by 2.3 percent, or about $12 billion."[1] One individual, behaving badly, affected the bottom line of half a dozen large firms by 2.3 percentage points. That was a huge effect wrought by one individual's personal influence.

Tiger Woods was, and still is a role model, albeit damaged goods, and he is still involved in the repair of his reputation and redemption of his image. He is making great progress. In the October 2019 issue of *Economist* magazine, in three very well executed photographs, he posed as the winner of his fifth Masters' Golf Tournament and the fifteenth major victory of his career. On his wrist was a lovely *Rolex Deepsea* model watch. Their advertising mantra is, "Every Rolex tells a story."[2] Tiger is once again endorsing the *Rolex* brand, this time the *Deepsea*

Perpetual model. Rolex has a market value of around $9 billion dollars. That is a lot of trust to earn back from stockholders and officers of a major corporation.

On the plus side, he has consistently been involved in the *TGR Foundation* he established 22 years ago. This is an organization dedicated to helping minority and underprivileged young people achieve great scholastic results. They have assisted some 175,000 children over the years. The foundation was in the background as his scandals unfolded, and it was negatively impacted at the time. By 2019 however, it was once again receiving donations from many affluent individuals and *Fortune 500* firms. To date, some $105 million dollars have been raised, and 15 cities have sponsored major events. His work with *TGR Foundation* is one reason why people would want to, once again, follow Tiger Woods. He has showed that despite the dreadful upheaval, the loss of income and reputation, it is possible to come back—and accomplish a lot of good in the process.

Tiger has returned to the game of golf and has won a series of tournaments, despite back surgery and other daunting physical challenges. This determined athlete continued training, using physical therapy, and found ways to overcome severe pain and perform once again with excellence. He displays dedication, perseverance, and grit—all necessary and desired traits in a leader. It is possible to recover from failure and thrive, once again. It took ten years of personal development, humility, self-examination, and growth—emotionally and mentally. Tiger shows it was worth the effort, and that rewards are still available for hard work and learning from past failures.

Sometimes recovery is not so forthcoming, and the choices that lead to a loss of credibility also lead to a loss of leadership, marriage, money, and personal freedom. We do incredibly silly things—commit criminal acts or put on a false front to impress people. It makes us feel better about ourselves and gives temporary status. On *Facebook*, dating sites, and other social media, we use photos from twenty years ago when we were younger, more attractive—and much thinner. Dave Ramsey has a saying, and it just so true: "We buy things we don't need with money we don't have to impress people we don't like."

Edward Rostohar: Twelve Years in Prison

Edward Rostohar, former CEO of the CBS Employees Federal Credit Union, is a sad example of a fallen leader. He will be incarcerated for at least the next dozen years. He stole $40 million and concealed this embezzlement for more than twenty years. He was able to do so by exploiting weaknesses in the audit system of the *National Credit Union Association*. As a former *NCUA* auditor, prior to his stint as Credit Union CEO, he learned various methods of theft and concealment as part of his audit training to *combat* theft. He was later able to use this same knowledge to conceal his crimes.[3]

Criminal irony.

When Rostohar was the CEO, he led a team of financial and banking professionals. He deliberately lied to his staff for decades, concealing his criminal activities. Imagine their sense of betrayal about being deceived and lied to? They may even feel responsible for the severe financial losses credit union customers incurred. The financial damage to savings accounts and checkbooks is just the beginning. The pain to his subordinates, to their emotions, self-esteem, and credibility is tremendous. It will be very hard for some of them to recover from his selfish actions.

His crimes took place over several decades. Mr. Rostohar used the illusion of wealth to attract younger women, to woo and impress them. Currently, he is in his 60s, and his wife of just a few years, Linda Bella, is in her 20s. She is young and attractive. Born in France, she is currently pursuing a career as a musician and actress here in the United States. According to an affidavit prepared by the FBI, after they were married for several years he began giving his wife a weekly allowance of $5,000 for acting lessons and other expenses.[4]

It is a sad story of love gone terribly wrong, greed, and living extravagantly. The credibility of the person in the position of leadership at any financial institution is vitally important. Without integrity and transparency, there can be no trust. This is also a case of poor leadership on the part of the Board of Directors. They did not hold the CEO accountable and did not perform random and routine checks of the financial statements. They either ignored or did not notice what should have been obvious and blatant right in front of them. How could someone on his salary afford the lifestyle he and his spouse were enjoying? The blame is squarely on the Board of Directors for their neglect and failure to hold their CEO accountable, and also on the former CEO for his criminal acts. The result is a bankrupt institution, devastated former employees, and clients of the credit union who are also suffering severe financial losses, possibly even bankruptcy.

Mr. Rostohar will be spending at least 12 years in prison, and his wife's weekly allowance has gone away. It was reported that he used embezzled funds to buy expensive watches, vehicles, several upscale homes, as well as paying for trips for various attractive young women to international locations. In the sentencing memorandum, the prosecutor for the government wrote, "(Rostohar) has the moral culpability of someone who was willing to leave as many as 43 depositors with deep losses so that he could wear $100,000 watches, buy a new vehicle every couple years, and impress women less than half his age with trips on private jets to international vacation resorts, *Tiffany* jewelry, and gambling parties."[5]

This kind of news is too prevalent in our society today. How many times do we hear reports like the one about the local little league treasurer being arrested for embezzling funds from the league bank account? The parents and boosters of the little league either did not suspect or ignored the signs of a problem. The youth pastor at church is in a sexual relationship with one of his students. A school resource officer is found to have child pornography on his work computer. The campaign finance manager for a politician is found to have been illegally soliciting campaign funds. These things happen too often and they never fail to ruins lives and tarnish reputations.

These kinds of things would occur much less often, if competent leadership employed a consistent and diligent set of accountability measures.

Credibility Matters

This is why leadership is so vital. It does not matter if it is the local Boy Scout troop or the multibillion-dollar firm of *Enron* or the campaign finances of our senator or president. The results are the same. John Maxwell is 100% correct: "everything rises and falls on leadership." In a *Facebook* post on November

15, 2015, he said, "Credibility is a leader's currency. With it, he or she is solvent; without it, he or she is bankrupt." Many male pastors and leaders of all denominations, including our former Vice President, have employed the "Billy Graham" policy. This is a personal policy decision where a man will avoid being alone with a female who is not their wife or family member. This includes business meetings, travel, meals, and any such occasion where appearances could be misconstrued. It may be considered controversial, but it does prevent difficulty and accusations regarding illicit sexual advances or encounters. Billy Graham desired to "Abstain from all *appearance of evil.* ..." as written in 1 Thessalonians 5:22.

Credibility can be partially built upon skill and policy but to flesh it out and fulfill it, we have to walk it out, live and in person. Billy Graham founded the *ECFA*, the *Evangelical Council for Financial Accountability*. Many non-profit organizations use their *Seven Standards of Responsible Stewardship* as a guideline for developing policies and procedures for financial transactions and recordkeeping. One such policy many churches and ministries use is that any individual who is actively involved in handling cash, checks, deposits or funds of any kind will take a five-day consecutive vacation/leave each year.

This simple yet powerful accountability measure is a policy, thus it is not personally aimed at any one individual and should not cause offense. If there is resistance to the requirement, that can be the first sign of difficulty that should be investigated. Common sense is still a very powerful tool in fighting fraud, crime, and illuminating other poor choices or actions that may impact an organization.

Leaders must truly lead by building, developing, and walking out the attributes of great leadership—the foremost being credibility. Great leaders will employ wisdom and common sense to make sure accountability measures are in place. This protects the leader and the organization from much difficulty. Our beloved President Ronald Reagan had a famous saying, "Trust but verify." The best leaders keep in mind that their highest priority is to protect the organization and those they serve.

Failing at something is not always a bad thing. Failure causes us to look at our actions, reconsider our choices, and review the circumstances that led to the day at hand. Failure helps us learn and is also necessary for us to grow forward."
— Bruce Gimbel

"Failures, repeated failures, are finger posts on the road to achievement."
— C.S. Lewis

Chapter Seven: What is Failure?

Would you trust your future retirement to a financial planner who inadvertently lost money for his clients? Or the crucial hit to a baseball player with a poor batting average? Nobody today has a .406 average like Ted Williams did in 1941, but you still need more wins than losses to successfully maintain a sports team or a financial planning practice. In most areas where great rewards are sought, there is a measure of risk-taking involved. Ball players have been badly injured executing the finest play of their career. Mickey Mantle twisted his leg in a center field drain pipe at Yankee Stadium in the 1951 World Series. He was 19-years-old, and injuries plagued the superstar thereafter throughout his career. He could have been even greater than he was. Occasionally, investors are impacted by circumstances beyond their control.

Deepwater Horizon

Our family has a financial planner who does a terrific job for us. He is incredibly honest and transparent. When we were brand new clients, he disclosed how he had recommended that a client buy *BP (British Petroleum)* stock on April 19, 2010. This was the day before the *Deepwater Horizon* industrial oil spill disaster began, discharging almost five million barrels of oil into the Gulf of Mexico.

Our financial planner had no way of knowing the *Deepwater Horizon* event was going to occur. He was using solid data and cumulative recommendations from highly regarded industry sources when he making the recommendation to his client. Nevertheless, because of his own personal integrity, the high standards of his employer, and the financial industry regulatory requirements, he routinely discloses this information. What happened may have discouraged a few prospective clients from signing up with him but my family has never regretted our decision. We recommend him to our friends, other family members, and business associates. He is a trusted advisor who watches our nest egg as through it were his very own. He has a high level of competency and professional expertise and has proven himself to be an excellent financial advisor.

I want to strongly emphasize that I do not consider that he failed his clients at any time, in any way, regarding the *BP* oil spill event. Sometimes things happen over which we have no control, even when we strive to make the best decisions based on the most advantageous information available at the time. In the context of what my friend Bruce says, our planner was able to "*look at his actions, reconsider his choices, and review the circumstances that led to the day at hand.*"

The failure for the *Deepwater Horizon* oil spill is shared by several large entities who failed to recognize there was a problem and ignored opportunities to correct things *before* the disaster. They further neglected to put in place sufficient safety policies and disaster recovery procedures. That was the real failure. Too often, we hold innocent people responsible for unfortunate events that are ultimately caused and made worse by the failures of other leaders or organizations.

President Obama formed *The National Commission on the BP Deepwater Horizon Oil Spill and Offshore Drilling* in May 2010. The final report was issued in January 2011, and stated that the commission "attributed the spill to a lack of regulatory oversight by the government and negligence and time-saving measures on the part of *BP* and its partners. *BP* had employed several firms, including *Halliburton* and *Transocean* to perform installation and maintenance of various portions of the drilling rig and platform, including concrete seals and caps to plug various parts of the drilling apparatus."[1]

Further investigation by the Joint Investigation Team of the *Bureau of Ocean Energy Management, Regulation and Enforcement (BOEMRE)* and the *U.S. Coast Guard* concluded that **BP was ultimately responsible for the spill**. Their final report by noted that, "although the defective concrete cap had been installed by Halliburton, decisions about the installation process made by *BP* had been the cause of the failure. The investigation further found that *BP* and *Transocean* employees aboard the rig had—while engaged in testing procedures—ignored early indications of a problem and thus missed opportunities to prevent a full-scale blowout."[2]

Our financial advisor was not responsible for the blowback on their stock prices following the disaster of the *Deep-Water Horizon BP* failure. He did, however, take the opportunity to look at each part of the process he uses to evaluate financial products and services offered to his clientele. His firm took the time to ascertain if there was a way to improve awareness, to be helpful to their clients in gaining insight and information, and perhaps using data more efficiently. Overall, many individuals and firms examined the fallout from this event and looked at how to avoid future exposure. They learned from the situation, adjusted their view, and moved forward.

Adjusting our view, and adapting to a "new reality" is a critical part of leadership. We cannot stagnate or get stuck in the mud and weeds. We must adapt while looking backward *and* forward. In my own life, I had to take a time of deep reflection to reevaluate my vocation and adjust my thinking about success and failure.

After working in the same industry for more than thirty years (the final few years on a part time basis), I retired in 2014. Retirement left me with a sense of failure. It was as though I had wasted a lot of years not doing anything significant. When people work hard in their career, hopefully there is a meaningful sense of accomplishment at the end. I was going to try to volunteer, but it felt like I had nothing to offer. My experience was insufficient. Volunteering is supposed to help keep one mentally sharp, is purportedly good for emotional health, and keeps one socially active and has physical benefits, as well. I did some volunteer work.

But I only smiled on the outside.

Some of my peers retired and used their professional network and expertise to become consultants and entrepreneurs. They were still earning income and being useful and relevant in the industry. Measured against the accomplishments of my peers, I thought I had pretty much failed. I moped around for a while feeling pretty miserable until I discovered something vital.

> I was looking through the wrong end of the binoculars.

Wrong End of the Binoculars

Instead of measuring and evaluating what I had learned and accomplished over thirty plus years, I was diminishing and devaluing my accomplishments. A good friend invited me to volunteer again, and I said yes. I also enrolled in college once again. Eventually, I started to see that I was looking at my life, career, and accomplishments incorrectly. If I was viewing my life through binoculars, I was looking through the wrong end.

It turned out I had developed some fine skills, such as negotiation and the ability to quickly and accurately diagnose and assess costs. I discovered skills in volunteer and vendor acquisition and other competencies. I had acquired a nice repertoire of soft skills, such as critical and creative thinking, decision making, the ability to recognize and interpret social cues and nuances, empathy, networking, and how to deploy them in the business and non-profit environment.

Soft skills are attributes used when a person solves problems, resolves conflicts, and interacts in relationships with clients, peers, subordinates, and others. These are necessary skills for successful leadership on and off the job. As I continued to study and learn, it became apparent that I had not wasted my career and previous time in college. Instead, it helped me become a useful, enthusiastic, and creative team member who could also lead, decide, and make worthwhile contributions in a second career. It felt great to realize I still had potential and value.

Everyone goes through low spots, questioning their worth, recovering from negative or unkind remarks and the inevitable failures that come into our lives. How we respond to these events is part of developing leadership skills through the process of getting to know yourself. Remember, you must know and lead yourself first before you can lead others well. Leadership professors James Kouzes and Barry Posner write, "The quest for leadership, therefore, is first an inner quest to discover who you are, and it's through this process of self-examination that you find the awareness needed to lead. Self-confidence is really awareness of and faith in your own powers, and these powers become clear and strong only as you work to identify and develop them. The mastery of the art of leadership comes with the mastery of the self, and so developing leadership is a process of developing the self."[3]

Developing a healthy way to view ourselves is very important. The illustration about looking through the wrong end of the binoculars was particularly helpful to me. Binoculars are basically two telescopes placed side by side and held in place with a fixed bridge or connector. There are a great deal of scientific and mathematical applications that go into designing, testing, and manufacturing binoculars, but the simple version of how they work can be understood by the layman.

The eyepiece lens is the small end, consisting of two magnification lenses, concave in nature, lined up one in front of the other. The large end, the viewing end, is the objective lens, which is convex, domelike in nature. When we view a distant object, and light rays pass through the objective lens, the convex lens, the light rays bend and cross over and sometimes appear to be upside down when viewed through the concave magnification lenses. Binoculars have a pair of prisms inside the barrel that enable correction of the image to be viewed with our human eyes. In effect the prisms rotate or flip the image for proper viewing. If we look at objects through the wrong end, we will see distorted and malformed images.

Most of us are curious, creative, and even sometimes childlike, so if gifted with a telescope or set of binoculars, it is natural to experiment and look through both ends to see what happens. Looking through the large, objective lens (the wrong end) produces a result that is both distorted and distant. Everything viewed through the wrong end appears tiny and insignificant, perhaps almost invisible, even when adjusting the lens viewer knob. This magnification and diminishment of images may be just silly fun when engaging in a children's game, but there is a real possibility this action could be significant in medical settings and psychological applications.

A small study of biology and pain effects was conducted in 2008 at Oxford University in Great Britain. Patients looking at magnified images of their limb experienced a result called "inverted binocular phenomenon" or *Disowning Pain Phenomenon*. Essentially, the larger the image of their right arm, the limb where they were experiencing chronic pain, the higher the pain level they reported. The opposite was also true, When the image of their arm was smaller, so was the pain level. They saw their arm through a pair of binoculars where the size of the image (their arm) was magnified and diminished over several iterations of the experiment. The researchers concluded that "the obvious clinical implication is that if manipulation of visual input can reduce the pain and swelling evoked by movement, it may assist in the rehabilitation of acute and chronic physical, neurological and psychiatric disorders associated with certain body image disturbances."[4]

Looking at our lives through the wrong end of the binoculars yields a distorted and inaccurate view of our accomplishments and value. It can warp our self-esteem and cause emotional pain and suffering. Being aware of these dangers helps us keep a healthy and balanced view of our lives. We can see where work is necessary on the parts that need improvement, and we can celebrate the parts that are doing well. We can speak to ourselves, encourage and coach ourselves, even in times when there is no cheerleading squad present. Everyone feels alone and on their own from time to time. So, it is important to maintain a healthy view, adjust to the reality of the situation, and adapt to move forward.

A lot of women (men, too) can tell you how much better they feel when they shed excess weight, even as little as five or ten pounds. The more appealing, attractive visual image they see in the mirror can be the jumpstart for better health. Success begets success, and every journey starts with the first step. How many times have we heard of setbacks where you eat cookies, ice cream, or potato chips and then beat yourself up over the weight gained back during a temporary loss of self-control? This is especially problematic right now given the restrictions and lockdowns for covid-19 and the resultant mental health issues from loneliness and isolation.

Is that failure? Should I just quit and not even try? Or is it better to think of it as just a temporary situation, a bump in the road and forgive yourself? Put your feet back on the correct path, resist the carb genie by distracting yourself with a walk, a short meditation session, or even a phone call to a friend. The methodology of positive self-talk or calling a friend when you are tempted to drink, do drugs, eat carbs, or harm yourself, all works in the same way. Most 12-step recovery programs emphasize this. You feel alone, desperate, and out of control. By speaking calmly and positively to yourself, encouraging, and comforting yourself, you can interrupt the pattern. Self-talk or connecting with a friend are great ways to interrupt the cycle of desperation and loneliness to begin gathering strength and renewed will power.

It turns out how we think and speak (to ourselves and others) is powerful and makes a huge difference in failure or success. Thinking about the same situation in a different way is a process that enables us to recognize and even appreciate the positive parts of our dilemma. Our grandmothers used to call it "finding the silver lining" in a situation. Experts today refer to it as "reframing" our perspective. We find the positive aspects, the better parts of a situation and choose to be grateful for them. Grateful plus attitude = gratitude.

Change Your Perspective

I recall a time when I was deeply sad for several months about a situation that seemed to be a failure—and it *was* my fault. After the fact, I found out other people had not even registered the event, let alone considered it a failure, but to me it had grown to monumental proportions. We do that to ourselves. Zig Ziglar calls it "stinkin' thinkin'." On a particularly bad day I found a televised church service where Joel Osteen was preaching about *changing your perspective*. He gave a simple list of accurate and hard-hitting facts that describe the blessings and good fortune enjoyed by the average American. These are a few I remember:

- "If you have $15 in your pocket, you are rich! You have more money than 3.5 billion people in the world."
- "If you live in America, you probably have more than one TV in your house as well as indoor plumbing and air conditioning; that's more than 4 billion people in the world have."
- "Last night you were probably one of 85% of people in the US that got to pick what you wanted to eat for supper. You have choices and options my friend."

In less than twenty minutes, my mood was considerably brighter. I felt much better. It started to be embarrassing that I was wallowing in self-pity, because I had it "so good" and was so blessed. I wrote down and repeated things on the list and it made a big difference over the next few days.

It was a ***tremendous*** life lesson.

Gratitude can change your perspective about everything. This situation occurred in 2006, and I have used the strategy numerous times to shake off the *mullygrubs*. One time, I changed it up a little and started to count the comfort and personal hygiene items in my bathroom. I wrote them all down and thanked God out loud for each item, for toothpaste, a toothbrush, soap, shampoo, toilet paper, petroleum jelly, and so on until the count reached fifty-five items. It does change your perspective when you stop to think that we may have fifty-five items in our bathrooms that we take for granted every day. These are things that are so lacking in other people's lives all over the globe. It can be a real eye opener and a cure for the blues.

This "reframing" is a sharp and useful tool for cutting away self-pity and a warped view of our circumstances. But you may have to reframe more than a few times. Soon after my session with the *mullygrubs*, I saw a televised advertisement for a well-known brand of petroleum jelly used in topical application to assist healing in various skin and wound conditions. The firm that manufactures and sells this product launched the "Healing Project" in 2015, where they partnered with a non-profit organization called *Direct Relief*. They distribute their products to assist those suffering from poverty, skin diseases, and other conditions.

They have helped more than 1.3 million people in the United States and nearly 5 million people globally. In addition to a lack of water, food, and shelter, skin diseases and conditions are a barrier to good health and productive lives. We just do not think about the deep implications of skin disease and how welcome a tube of petroleum jelly can be. We are fortunate to have options and choices when we get to:

- Drive to the store most any time of the day or night *we choose*
- View the options of petroleum jelly products and what *we prefer*
- *Choose* the product we want and *pay* for it with no problem or questions
- Drive home and use the product *as we see fit* to heal our skin condition

Oprah Winfrey, on her award-winning television talk show, made famous five simple words, "have an attitude of gratitude." This is powerful and meaningful. She insists it will change your life for the better if you truly cultivate the attitude and spirit of what it means. Dr. Robert Emmons, Professor of Psychology at the University of California supports her theory. He is the author of a new book entitled, *Thanks! How The New Science of Gratitude Can Make You Happier,* and he has been researching gratitude for over a decade. He has discovered that life can be quite improved with the development and practice of gratitude. He writes, "Without gratitude, life can be lonely, depressing, and impoverished. Gratitude enriches human life. It elevates, energizes, inspires, and transforms; and those who practice it will experience significant improvement in several areas of life including relationships, academics, energy level, and even dealing with tragedy and crisis."

His research has shown there are many physical, psychological, and social benefits derived from a spirit and attitude of gratitude. In an article entitled "Why Gratitude is Good" he elaborates on four specific points:

- Gratitude allows us to celebrate the present by magnifying positive emotions. It helps us appreciate the value of something or someone and we then are less likely to take it for granted.
- Gratitude helps block envy, regret and other negative emotions. Research published in a 2008 study by psychologist Alex Wood, in the *Journal of Research in Personality*, explains gratitude can positively affect individuals experiencing depression by reducing the frequency and duration of episodes.
- Grateful people are more stress resistant. In the face of serious trauma, adversity, and suffering, if people have a grateful disposition, they may recover more quickly.
- Grateful people have a higher sense of self-worth. He thinks there is a sense of well-being where others have helped you get to an improved place in life. [5]

Was It Really Failure?

The symptoms of failure can show up in various ways and be solved by employing some creative and effective methods. A Canadian study of adults who tried to quit smoking shows it may ultimately take up to ***thirty attempts before successfully quitting***. I'm like Michael Jordon; I failed 9,000 times, time after time, before I finally succeeded and was able to quit smoking for good. I've been fortunate to have zero relapses since I quit ten years ago. However, I am aware that if I have even one cigarette, I may not lay them down again. I'm a recovering *smokaholic*, period.

When I quit smoking, I took up carbs. I will "carb out" on occasion, so I'm still working on portion control for crackers and bread. Is that considered a "failure" in the carb department? Did I fail overall because I substitute carbs for cigarettes? Should I even look at the situation this way? I answer that with a resounding NO!!! I simply won't wrestle with it that way because crackers are infinitely better for me than cigarettes.

That is a form of success in and of itself. I can't breathe deeply or walk fast for exercise if I continue to smoke, but I can if I eat crackers. It's not perfect, but it's definitely a huge movement forward. That's what reframing is about. We look at the situation at hand, view it in a positive light, and glean the best possible outcome at that time. My next goal is portion control in the carbohydrate family, and I will get there. Reaching the ten-year mark on victory over smoking gives me confidence and optimism in other areas of my life.

Success builds on success.

A crazy, but healthy, friend runs the occasional marathon, but I guarantee you he did not wake up one morning and decide to run a marathon the next day. There are stretching and breathing exercises involved, protein eating schedules, hydration methods, and wearing out many pairs of running shoes. He trains for a minimum of several months. It takes discipline and perseverance to even prepare for a marathon, let alone run in one. He may "fail" by not finishing first, but let's say he trains well and runs fast enough to finish in the top five. Is that considered a "failure" since he did not place first?

Does that mean that all other participants should quit running or should they say, "Wow! I have improved so much. Last time I ran a marathon I finished twentieth and now I'm in the top five!" If he looks at the race from a wider perspective, he can say that out of 200 people in the marathon, he finished in the top five. If he uses the experience as an opportunity to examine his routines and habits, he can find areas to change, improve and tweak for even better success next time. That's a much healthier perspective.

In viewing failure, we may wish to look deeper at what is and is not a failure. There are only 500 firms in the *Fortune*

500, therefore only 500 CEOs. Many more men and women aspire to those positions, but if only 500 can achieve them, should no one else study, work, train, dream, and try to attain one of those rare positions? Are those who do not achieve that accomplishment and title considered to be failures? It is more accurate and certainly a healthier view to say there are many people training to fill future positions in those firms, including that of CEO. We do not cease to apply for jobs, yearn for a better life, quit running marathons, or bury our dreams just because someone else finished in first place or was hired into the top position.

There is not a human being on earth who has not failed at something, and most fail more than once or twice. Stories abound about famous people and their initial failures and subsequent successes, the before and after:

> *I've learned that it doesn't matter how many times you failed. You only have to be right once. I tried to sell powdered milk. I was an idiot lots of times, and I learned from them all. Sweat equity is the best start-up capital.*[6]
> —*Mark Cuban*

Steven Spielberg was rejected twice when he tried to enroll in film school at University of Southern California (USC). Yet, Spielberg has grossed more than eight *billion* dollars from his films. After he became famous and successful, he was ironically awarded an honorary degree and became a trustee of the same university.

Michael Jordan was cut from his high school varsity basketball team in his sophomore year. In a *YouTube* video entitled *Michael Jordon on Failure*, he says "I've missed more than 9,000 shots in my career. I've lost almost 300 games. Twenty-six times, I've been trusted to take the game winning shot and missed. I've failed over and over and over again in my life. And that is why I succeed."

It took five years and 5,126 failed prototypes for Sir James Dyson to develop the world's first bagless vacuum cleaner. Ten years later, he is the top vacuum cleaner designer and manufacturer. He sells more vacuums than anyone else in the world. Sir James has a seven billion dollar net worth today.

What we did not see or hear was how many times Mark Cuban or Steven Spielberg looked for answers, read articles, asked questions, and reflected on their failures. They obviously learned from them and kept moving forward, in spite of being an idiot selling powdered milk, being rejected, or disillusioned. We don't see Michael Jordan practicing the same shot a thousand times, smell his sweat, or see his worn-out sneakers as he kept practicing and shooting. Nor do we know how many thousands of hours James Dyson spent in the lab, exhausted, frustrated, and disappointed. We do know they all persevered because we now see the self-evident results of their success.

If we give ourselves credit for our own sweat, perseverance and grit, it will be easier to move forward. We should have an accurate, healthy view of our flaws, abilities, and accomplishments, to assess how we can change and improve. Just because we all have unique talents and gifts, we are not all meant to do the same thing or end up in the same place. For instance, I have no talent for engineering or inventing, but I am very good at using a vacuum cleaner and content to leave the engineering to Mr. Dyson as he continues to improve his product line.

Jeff Stibel is an author, journalist, partner in Bryant Stibel as well as Vice Chairman of the prestigious powerhouse *Dun and Bradstreet*. He received a Brain and Behavior Fellowship while studying for his Masters' at *Brown University* and was awarded an honorary PhD from *Pepperdine University*. In *C-Suite Quarterly Web Magazine* he has written a series of articles entitled "Profiles in Failure." Included are the stories of Jeff Bezos, J. K. Rowling, Michael Jordan, and Warren Buffett. All of these successful people suffered epic failures before ultimate success in sports, business, and media. They are worth a closer look for encouragement, and so we can be reminded that most of us fail often before we succeed.

"There are no secrets to success. It is the result of preparation, hard work, and learning from failure."
— *Colin Powell*

"Success is a continuing thing. It is growth and development. It is achieving one thing and using that as a steppingstone to achieve something else."
— *John C. Maxwell*

Chapter Eight: What is Success?

Classic View

Colin Powell and John Maxwell are examples of success. Powell was promoted many times during his 35 years of military service, eventually reaching the rank of four-star General in the United States Army. But he didn't stop there. He went on to serve with distinction as National Security Advisor, Chairman of the Joint Chiefs of Staff, and Secretary of State. John Maxwell is an author, speaker, and leader, who achieved notable success by writing more than 40 best-selling books. He is a highly-regarded and sought after consultant in the international business community.

Franklin Graham and Rick Warren are successful leaders of evangelical ministries. Jaime Dimon and Warren Buffett are successful leaders in the financial community, having enriched their staff members and stockholders. Bill Gates, Steve Jobs, and many other titans of the tech industry have led their companies to success through difficulties and legal challenges––even stockholder rebellion. This is the *classic view* of success, climbing the corporate ladder to the corner office, enjoying the accolades and financial rewards of years of hard work and sacrifice.

Skewed View

People often define success in personal ways, and they have a variety of goals. Many years ago, I worked in an office with a young man who had a singular and consistent goal for success. He would literally repeat "50K" over and over to himself, and sometimes others. It was code for the goal of earning $50,000 a year. He never spoke of any of other goal. He did not have a specific plan to achieve his goal, but he believed hard work would get him to his goal. I do not remember his name and just vaguely recall his physical appearance. Yet his definition of success and his determination to get there has stuck with me and I truly believe he achieved his goal.

There was another young woman in that same office almost thirty years ago. She was married, with one child. The family lived a modest home with no mortgage. She had inherited the home from her grandmother. She was always meticulous her appearance, very well groomed, and always fashionably attired. We became friends and our families started to socialize together. She later confided to me that they had severe financial problems—particularly large credit card debt, mostly from clothing purchases, entertainment and dining expenses. It was very important to live the lifestyle as much as possible until they arrived at the desired address of perceived success. .

My friend and her husband were not satisfied with a mortgage free home—she wanted much more. She had a dream that was out of reach. She desperately wanted to live in Bayshore, an affluent enclave dotted with expensive homes. Wanting this so badly, she would drive up and down Bayshore Boulevard in the middle of the night, imagining what it would be like to live in one of the grand houses overlooking the bay. I actually rode along with her on several occasions to see what her dream was all about. I tried to be sympathetic and listen as she spoke about her deep desire. She affirmed her goal often and with as much fervor as the young man who wanted to earn "50K."

Her family was already poised for success,. After all, they were better off than so many others, having the great advantage of owning a mortgage-free. They could have reduced their expenses and saved for an early retirement, college for their, son or some other reasonable goal. But based on their income range, the Bayshore home was not a realistic goal. In addition, it was the dream of only one partner in the marriage—her husband was not interested in living on the Bayshore.

Eventually, this discontent created tension in their marriage. They drifted apart, eventually divorcing and finding new partners. I get sad when I remember my friend. She had an unrealistic and dream. In the Book of Proverbs there is great wisdom about this: "Remove far from me vanity and lies: give me neither poverty nor riches; feed me with food convenient for me."[1]

Temporary Success Through Deceit

In 2015, Carlos Ghosn, an automobile executive born in Brazil but holding French and Lebanese citizenship, was the CEO of Japanese automaker, *Nissan*, as well as head of the European manufacturer, *Renault*. At that time, he oversaw ten percent of the global automobile market. According to an article in *Time Magazine*, his nicknames were "Le Cost Killer" and "Mr. Fix It" because he was able to guide *Nissan* back from the verge of bankruptcy in 1999 to good financial health. During the years 2000-2005 he received accolades, such as being one of the top ten most influential business leaders in the world. At the peak of his career, he awarded was the CEO of two Fortune 500 firms, a position few have achieved.[2]

But by 2017, signs of trouble were emerging. There were reports of *Nissan* was using uncertified technicians for inspections and missing quality control targets. There were recalls and production stopped. Mr. Ghosn had overspent on marketing and media events. And he used $200 million of company money to help sponsor the 2016 Olympic Games in Rio de Janerio. He also used millions to acquire questionable real estate holdings, thinly veiled as corporate housing when he travelled to France, Brazil, and other countries.

Financial audits soon revealed much more.

Fast forward to 2019, and Ghosn was indicted in Japan for misappropriating funds for personal enrichment, conspiracy, and fraud. He was arrested and spent several months in a 10 x16 foot cell with restricted visitors, no furniture, and dismal prospects for bail. He believed this was revenge from *Nissan* and is—at least in part—because he is a foreigner. Later that year, he was transferred out of the holding cell and placed on house detention. He orchestrated an elaborate escape plan and fled to Lebanon where he now lives in exile. He is skeptical that he could receive a fair trial in Japan and has no plans to return. Lebanon does not have an extradition treaty with Japan. Ghosn's future is uncertain.[3]

In 2015, Martin Winterkorn, CEO of *Volkswagen AG*, was lauded as a leading CEO. He kept his firm viable and successful, even though the 2008 global recession. He had been the CEO since 2007, and he was also the Chairman of the Board of Management at *Audi AG*, a subsidiary of *Volkswagen*. Winterkorn came to that role back in 2002 and originally joined Volkswagen in 1993.

In 2014, the scandal regarding diesel emissions fraud came to light and the next year Winterkorn resigned as CEO of Volkswagen but denied that he had knowledge of the emissions software fraud. In September 2015, *Volkswagen* admitted they had cheated on emissions tests for at least six years. To date, this has cost that company more than $35 billion dollars in penalties and fees as well as untold billions in market share, not to mention goodwill. They have spent at least $25 billion in the United States alone to settle consumer claims.

It came out that Martin Winterkorn knew the diesel emission readings were being skewed, allegedly as early as 2014, but he did not alert authorities, keeping buyers in the dark. All this, while he was being lauded by *Forbes Magazine* as the 58th most powerful person in the world. In their short summary about Mr. Winterkorn, they said:

As chair of the Volkswagen Group, Martin Winterkorn urged European regulators not to overburden the automotive industry with excessive emission targets, citing a lack of time to develop fuel-efficient technology and the economic downturn as major concerns. The topic is especially close to Winterkorn, who vowed to make the company the biggest electric carmaker in the world and put 1 million electric vehicles on the road by 2020. The German automaker—whose brands include Volkswagen, Audi, Bentley, and Lamborghini—reported selling over 7.5 million vehicles this year and is close to achieving its goal of 10 million automobile sales in 2014.[4]

Winterkorn currently faces wire fraud and conspiracy charges in the United States, and in April 2019 Germany charged him with fraud, embezzlement, as well as the violation of competition laws. There are also allegations that he benefited from bonuses in the millions of dollars.[5]

Both Winterkorn and Ghosn had arrived at the pinnacle of success by choosing to cheat, lie, deceive, and cover up immoral, illegal, and unethical deeds and continue to enjoy the at least some of the poisoned fruit of their "success."

Healthy and Balanced view

Our friend Drew Dudley's attitude toward success is much more balanced and healthy. He says job titles and money are "the natural by-product of someone who adds tremendous value," and they are not terrific goals, "because we are not in charge of either of them…how much money you make….every promotion you get is someone else's decision." He consistently returns to the idea of knowing and leading ourselves well, and he describes himself as the CEO of his own life. "The most important role any of us will play is as CEO of our own lives. A CEO is responsible for the day-to-day activities of an organization, and their primary responsibility is to ensure the organization's health and growth. Most major organizations have a Board of Directors whose job it is to provide guidance and support to the CEO (our families, friends, and mentors), but it's our job as CEO of our own lives to make the decisions that keep ourselves happy and healthy."[6]

Drew has dealt with alcoholism, mental illness, obesity, and the loss of a beloved partner. Through it all, he has overcome and sustained success by employing a philosophy known as "This is Day One." If every day is Day One, "the key to success in each of them is to identify the key foundational decisions that have to occur on the first day of the journey and making sure you live them each day. What you'll be capable of on the 100th version of Day One will be significantly more impressive than on your 1st version, but each day must be treated like it's the first. It allows you to forgive yourself and start over after a screwup and keeps you from becoming complacent and forgetting the foundational behaviors that got you there when you achieve some success."[7]

For Drew, one great personal success was losing 100 pounds in a year. His health improved and his self-esteem increased. In fact, losing weight is a personal success for many people. In a *TEDx* talk in Anchorage, Alaska, he gave a 14-minute presentation on the culture of leadership and said success is being able to "define the things that define us." He challenged his audience to a game. If someone followed you around for two weeks, and you did not know they were tracking you, what three core values they would see in you? They would see everything you did and said, to whom you talked, how you spoke to them, and how you interacted—all day long. He urged them to define the values in a very basic way, so simple a four-year-old would understand.[8]

For example, for the value of respect, a simple definition might be "how I feel about someone, and how I treat them." You don't call people names or hit them, because you care about their feelings and their wellbeing. If I like someone, it is easier to be nice and "respectful." If they are troublesome, irritating, or rude—even if I just feel that they are rude or irritating—perhaps if I treat them well, it will make them feel better about themselves, and they will then treat others with more consideration. That fits nicely with John Maxwell's definition of success as "a continuing thing. It is growth and development. It is achieving one thing and using that as a steppingstone to achieve something else." Making someone feel better about themselves is always a checkmark in the success column.[9]

Drew finished his talk by sharing six questions he uses to develop himself and others each day. He says you must plan for success *and* failure. If you use the 300/365 and 4/6 rules, you build success into your day and account for the occasional failure. That way you already have a plan in place to do better. If you apply four of the six rules 300 out of 365 days a year, you will add 1,200 pieces of value to your life and the lives of others in your sphere of influence. His questions were designed to develop six personal core values:

- How have I recognized someone else's leadership today? (Impact)
- What have I done to make it more likely I will learn something? (Continuous Improvement)
- What have I done to make it more likely someone else will learn something? (Mentorship)

- What positive thing have I said about someone to their face today? (Empowerment)
- What positive thing have I said about someone who is not in the room? (Recognition)
- How have I been good to myself today? (Self-respect)[10]

Zig Ziglar, a consummate optimist, said, "Success occurs when opportunity meets preparation. The efforts that worked most often were encompassed in preparation. When I showed up knowing exactly what I was going to say to the prospect, showed up on time and ready for the coming conversation, showed up appropriately dressed and groomed—these things prepare the way for you to make a positive impression on your prospect with your knowledge and professionalism. And I can almost guarantee they will listen the next time you talk to them, too!"[11]

Another Ziglar definition for success is, "Success is the maximum utilization of the ability that you have" and to build on our abilities he urges us to "have persistent consistency. Consistency meaning that you work on your goal or objective every day or a least every week. Persistent meaning that when you are working on your goal you are always taking it up a notch, doing a little bit more, and learning a little bit more."[12]

Mr. Ziglar made these statements about success during an interview with *Forbes Magazine* contributor, Dan Schawbel.

He added one last piece of advice: "Honesty and integrity are absolutely essential for success in life—all areas of life. The really good news is that anyone can develop both honesty and integrity."[13] Zig provided a gracious invitation to those who need to improve and the opportunity to start the process of transformation.

A few Sundays ago, our church had a visiting pastor who told a story about when he was in seminary and worked part time at a funeral home. One of the men who worked there was grumpy, disagreeable—a complainer, always ready with negative comments about their boss. One day, the pastor decided that enough was enough and that he was going to say something to the chronic complainer.

He told the man he thought the boss had high hopes for him and that he must be very good at his job because he always got the top assignments. He also told him he thought the boss would eventually promote him to a top position and that would benefit the entire operation. These positive words seemed to work magic—immediately. The man stopped complaining so much and gradually started being positive, even more pleasant to work with. Like Mr. Ziglar, the visiting pastor provided an invitation, in a gracious and positive way, giving the man the opportunity to elevate his character and improve his circumstances.

Ziglar was a staunch Christian and a respected expert on what success really looks like, and how to be motived and successful while leading a balanced life. In his book *Born to Win!*, he said, "success cannot be defined in one sentence," but he insisted it is a compilation of many things. One could say the definition of success depends on the individual goals, experiences, and opportunities, as well as abilities and motivation. One size does not—and cannot—fit all. He also was very open and straightforward about his Christian beliefs and how he was deeply influenced by Biblical principles.

He is not alone in his quest for excellent leadership.

In February 2001, Coach John Wooden gave a *TEDx* talk in Monterey, California, where he spoke on the subject of True Success. A devout Christian, Wooden was known for his short and inspirational talks to his players. He spoke to them about success in basketball and, more important, success in *life*. In 1948, he published his *Pyramid of Success*, the culmination of more than two decades of work and research to pinpoint the top qualities necessary for success. His personal definition was, "Success is peace of mind, which is a direct result of self-satisfaction in knowing you made the effort to do your best to become the best that you are capable of becoming."[14] He was a lifelong learner. His books, some 25 in all, were bestsellers that provided insight into his coaching philosophy, views on life, leadership, success, and Christian values.

Fred Smith Sr. was an executive with *General Shoe Corporation*, *Gruen Watch Co.* and several other firms. He later opened *Fred Smith Associates*, a management consulting firm, that served *Mobil Oil*, *Caterpillar*, *Jefferson Standard Life Insurance* and other firms. He worked over sixty years and was respected as a wise and ethical man. Speaking and writing about success, he said he believed a man could have 10 million dollars and be wealthy, but not necessarily successful. Fred's definition was: "the person who's doing the most with what he's got is truly successful. Not the one who becomes the richest or most famous, but the one who has the closest ratio of talents received to talents used."[15]

Mr. Smith gave a speech in 1961 where he talked about the power of *principles*. In it, he shared a great quote about success: "I am convinced about one thing in regard to success. *No business ever owned success. We only lease success.* We cannot own it. There never comes a time when you can say, 'I am successful.' There comes a time when you can say, 'I am currently leasing success and the rent you pay on success is the commitment to thinking and doing. The lease is never prepaid nor paid up—the rent comes due year after year that you want to experience success.'"[16]

The question for this chapter has been, "What is success?" It is demonstrated in the examples of athletes who choose to work, sweat, putt, shoot thousands of hoops, or hit buckets of golf balls, to successfully improve their skills and eventually win the game. And it is demonstrated by Edward Rostohar, former CEO of the *CBS Credit Union* who was convicted of embezzlement. He was successful in his career, until he ceased to use wisdom, no longer practiced integrity, and lost his moral compass. He chose to embezzle money that was not his to maintain a lifestyle he could not afford, and he became morally bankrupt and lost his status, finances, and freedom. He was successful at failing miserably.

Top experts believe success is achieved through choices, hard work, perseverance, using wisdom, practicing integrity, and developing good moral character.

In other words—success is a choice *and* a result.

Failure, like death and taxes, will happen. Your response to failure holds the key to your future.
— John Maxwell

You know if a man falls down, he gets up again. And if a man goes the wrong way, he turns around and comes back.
— Jeremiah 8:4 (ERV)

Chapter Nine: Organizational Failure and Recovery

No one is immune from making poor choices that lead to failure. When we choose we are using personal moral values—our ideas of right and wrong. We develop these personal moral values through the influence of our parents, family, and other significant caregivers. Moral values help form our personal ethical eco-system and become our guiding principles. They help us evaluate situations, assess options, and choose actions or resolutions that uphold our ideals.

Each organization, as well, must develop its own core values and ethical code, which make a statement about the organization itself. These values should be endorsed by each member. This is where leadership comes in. A critical part of leading followers is to ensure the core values and ethical system align with the vision and goals of the organization.

Core values clearly define to clients, vendors, and employees what the organization stands for, as well as its priorities. Members use the ethical framework in the decision-making process, for building relationships, for serving clients, and in general representing the firm.

Let me share three examples. First, we first look at two well-known business leaders, their failures, and subsequent strategies for improvement and recovery. By examining these events, which give us insight into how leaders recover from failures, we can hopefully learn to avoid their mistakes.

The first step to recovery is getting out in front of the situation by admitting the error, taking responsibility, learning from it, and coming us with a plan to correct the failure. The next step is to move forward quickly, decisively, and in a transparent manner to execute the plan. Those who follow this strategy seem to be able to "lead *up* instead of step *out*," in the words of Jamie Dimon, CEO of *J. P. Morgan Chase*, which we will be see in the examples of Mr. Dimon and *Berkshire-Hathaway* CEO, Warren Buffett.

Problems and conflicts occur when core values are not upheld. For example, conflicts arise when the desire to make a profit is perceived to be stronger than the obligation to adhere to corporate values. Trading long-term good will for short-term profits is a poor strategy. Leadership failure in organizations with conflicting goals is difficult to correct. There may, in fact, be a legacy of deficiency in the Board of Directors.

Part One: Warren Buffett, CEO Berkshire Hathaway

Warren Buffett, popularly known as the "Oracle of Omaha," often consults with his close friend, Jamie Dimon. Mr. Buffett espouses the character traits held dear by Mr. Dimon such as hard work, transparency, integrity, learning from mistakes, treating others with respect and dignity, and taking care of both your employees and customers. Both recommend taking a long view and avoiding risky short term solutions. Both leaders use their annual stockholder letters and meetings to advise their shareholders about the progress and future plans of the companies they represent.

But they differ in their approach and methods.

Mr. Buffett has a weeklong meeting that is rather warm and folksy, compared to Mr. Dimon, who is more direct and pragmatic.[1] In his annual 2018 Letter to Stockholders, Mr. Buffett wrote about the culture and practice of leadership at *Berkshire Hathaway.*

For 54 years our managerial decisions at Berkshire have been made from the viewpoint of the shareholders who are staying, not those who are leaving. Consequently, Charlie and I have never focused on current-quarter results. Berkshire, in fact, may be the only company in the Fortune 500 that does not prepare monthly earnings reports or balance sheets. I, of course, regularly view the monthly financial reports of most subsidiaries. Our lack of such an instrument means that the parent company has never had a quarterly "number" to hit. Shunning the use of this bogey sends an important message to our many managers, reinforcing the culture we prize. Over the years, Charlie and I have seen all sorts of bad corporate behavior, both accounting and operational, induced by the desire of management to meet Wall Street expectations. What starts as an 'innocent' fudge in order to not disappoint 'the Street' – say, trade-loading at quarter-end, turning a blind eye to rising insurance losses, or drawing down a 'cookie-jar' reserve – can become the first step toward full-fledged fraud. Playing with the numbers 'just this once' may well be the CEO's intent; it's seldom the end result. And if it's okay for the boss to cheat a little, it's easy for subordinates to rationalize similar behavior.[2]

Both Buffett and Dimon advocate transparency and taking ownership of mistakes. They have both been willing to admit to, and accept the fallout of, those decisions. Warren Buffett missed two obvious and lucrative investment opportunities, namely, to purchase stock in *Google* and *Amazon*. At the annual Shareholders Meeting in 2017, he admitted that he "was too dumb to realize and also did not understand tech stocks," and did not buy stock in either firm. He has often said he "avoided tech stocks in the past because he didn't really understand how they were making money and whether they would be able to do so over the long term."

He has also been forthright about other poor business decisions. In his annual letters Buffett admits that he and his partner, Charlie Munger, have "missed a lot of things, and we'll keep doing it."[3] His willingness to admit failure, due to a lack understanding, and not taking advantage of opportunities, is part of why he remains a *trusted* leader of a exceedingly successful investment firm.

Mr. Buffett has made other poor choices, and to-date these have cost his investors over $15 billion in profits. In 1966, and again in 1995, he briefly owned and held shares in *The Walt Disney Company* and sold them less than two years later. Both times he made a profit, but not nearly as much as he would have if he had held the stock for 30 years as he has two others, *Coca-Cola* and *Wells Fargo*. Nonetheless, the real issue is whether or not we learn from our mistakes.

The answer for Buffett is *yes*.

Writing for the *Motley Food*, contributing author Sean Williams says:

> *The reality is that we're all going to be guilty of investing faux pas at some point in our lives. The key will be whether or not we learn from those mistakes. With more than seven decades of investing prowess now under his belt, Buffett has shown that he understands the value that can be created by purchasing and holding great companies. Of Berkshire's top 10 holdings, each has been held for an average of 7.5 years, demonstrating that Buffett has learned from his mistakes over the years.*[4]

Part Two: Jaime Dimon, CEO JP Morgan Chase

Dimon is the lone surviving financial services CEO and banker from the 2008 financial crisis, and he has learned much from those turbulent years. He recently signed a five-year extension on his contract to remain CEO, proving he is wiser in the wake of events that damaged his reputation. His credibility—or "leadership currency" as John Maxwell calls it—was bruised for a while. Maxwell says when we lose credibility we become *bankrupt* because we lose our followers. However, Mr. Dimon has successfully rebuilt his credibility after a series of errors.

Early in his career, Mr. Dimon would visit client sites to dig deep for information, places such as warehouses, construction sites, and other venues. He wanted to understand what worked and what did not—and why some clients could not pay back loans or how successful ones did. He insists that his team use these same practices today. He tells them, "Get the facts on the table. Share the facts. A balance sheet is not a hypothetical concept. How you treat people is not a hypothetical concept. Follow-up is not hypothetical."[5]

As an advocate of strong leadership, Dimon set forth the attributes he considers non-negotiable for a good leader. He is firm in his belief that in hard times great leaders step up, not out. And over the course of his career, Mr. Dimon has stepped up several times.

Mr. Dimon writes, "Leadership is an honor, a privilege, and a deep obligation. When leaders make mistakes, a lot of people can get hurt."[6] Avoiding self-deception and practicing empathy, clarity of thought, compassion, and strength of character makes a good leader. People will want to work for such leaders and they take time and effort to seek them out. *JP Morgan Chase* has been recognized by *Fortune Magazine* in the years 2015-2018 as the best megabank for employees, and by

Boston Consulting Group as the most innovative firm in 2016. For 23 years in a row the Chase firm has also been recognized as the best place to work for multicultural females and mothers, and has received many other "Best of" industry designations.[7]

Leaders work hard to build an idea, concept, organization, or network. They believe in something larger than themselves and are extremely loyal to their vision. No leader has all the answers or all the perfect traits, but Mr. Dimon strives for excellence. He says, "True leaders must set the highest standards of integrity—those standards are not embedded in the business but require conscious choices." People know when "he or she encounters the rare combination of emotional skill, integrity, and knowledge that makes a leader."[8]

As the leader, he takes the helm and the responsibilities very seriously, with a sharp focus on long term goals—not short-term profitability—to prop up the balance sheet. "Quarterly earnings—even annual earnings—frequently are the result of actions taken over the past five or 10 years," Dimon wrote in 2015.[9] His strategy includes greatly increased transparency to the Board of Directors, and to his staff and clients of the bank, especially after such a costly and humiliating failure.

He admits that his serious failures led to shareholder rumblings and temporary loss of confidence by most board members and government officials. The "London Whale" disaster of 2012 developed on Dimon's watch, when trader Bruno Iksil performed a series of risky derivative transactions involving credit default swaps (CDS). Dimon failed to monitor an inexperienced Chief Investment Officer, who in turn, failed to notice and stop the risky trading behavior of some traders in their London office. There was little corporate oversight and the Chief Risk Officer was also negligent in his lack of supervision of the risky investment practice involving CDS . Several other traders, including Javier Martin-Artajo and Julien Grout, were also accused of hiding millions of dollars in losses by marking positions at inflated prices.[10] By the end of the debacle, *J. P. Morgan Chase* had lost some $6.2 billion dollars and faced $700 million in fines from the *Security and Exchange Commission* (SEC).

Ironically, the risky CDS investment practice is what strongly contributed to the fall of insurance titan, *American International Group* (AIG), during the 2008 financial crisis, which came to be known as "The Great Recession". AIG lost more than $90 billion dollars in the near failure of a firm that had been dubbed "too big to fail." Initially, Dimon sought to downplay the crisis. In an April 2012 conference call, he called it, "a tempest in a teapot."

Less than a year later he accepted full responsibility. "Let me be direct," Dimon wrote to his 2013 letter to shareholders,

"The London Whale was the stupidest and most embarrassing situation I have ever been a part of."

According to analysis made by *Wharton School of Business* professor Peter Cappelli, "somewhere along the way, shareholders and management became acutely focused on improving efficiencies and short-term financial performance," A lack of proper staffing become a real part of the London Whale situation, with *JP Morgan Chase* not having a treasurer on staff for about five months and an inexperienced Chief Investment Officer overseeing traders and their transactions and risks.[11]

The company completely revamped its internal controls and policies, as well as its investment strategies. On the company's emergency conference call in April 2012, Dimon said that the strategy had been "flawed, complex, poorly reviewed, poorly executed, and poorly monitored." The trading disaster led to FBI and SEC investigations, severe market loss, as well as financial shockwaves that were felt globally. Serious questions were raided about of Dimon's leadership abilities, competency, and his lack of attention to personnel and policy details.

There were calls to strip him of the title of Chairman, and his 2013 income was cut by more than half. From this glaring failure he learned the importance of greater transparency and strengthening the oversight on traders and trades. He has since improved controls by implementing much closer scrutiny of complex transactions.

These measures help to restore the profitability and credibility of *JP Morgan Chase* and repair his own reputation. It was quite difficult and it took time, humility, and excruciating honesty with his staff, shareholders, and customers. He also had to reverse his previous position, where he objected to "the need for government regulations with regard to proprietary trading in large financial firms. We must not let regulatory reform and requirements create excessive bureaucracy and unnecessary permanent costs."[12]

The US Government, in fact, intervened after the debacle, moving to strengthen some regulations and adding others to repair the breech that allowed this disaster come almost undetected. They expanded SEC and FDIC oversight, where banks managing federally insured savings-and-checking deposit funds are required to limit risk and police their internal transactions to avoid the very thing that had happened. To avoid another such event, Dimon expanded his leadership sphere and invited others in his senior staff to police the risks, and share the spotlight.

In 2014, he invited five heads of various business units to write their own shareholder letters. This was a huge step for any leader and showed a willingness to be vulnerable and transparent. This rebuilt trust in his leadership. He gave this advice to others in his 2014 letter to shareholders:

> *Our goal is to think like a long-term investor — build great franchises, strengthen moats and have good through-the-cycle financial results. Achieve the benefits of scale and eliminate the negatives. Develop great long-term achievable strategies. And manage the business relentlessly, like a great operator. Finally, continue to develop excellent management that keeps it all going. As Thomas Edison said, 'Vision without execution is hallucination.'*"[13]

As proof of his recovery, Dimon accepted another five-year contract as CEO and Chairman. The board and the market believe he will lead them well in the future and that he has learned the lessons of the past.

Earlier in his career, he had been ousted as president of *Citigroup* by Chairman Sandy Weill, who later told the *New York Times* that he fired Dimon because he wanted to be CEO. Dimon had been at Citigroup for some 16 years. He had a reputation for arrogance and had become somewhat difficult, even approaching the verge of mutiny.[14] He was unhappy at being dismissed, but decided to go quietly.

He was given a handsome severance package and time to reflect and grow.

As he reflected on that ouster, Dimon admitted that he had made some mistakes and decided he was partly to blame. "One of his virtues as an executive is that he's blunt and truthful—to bosses, peers, and subordinates alike. He doesn't tend to mince words or spare people's feelings. As a younger man, when he was forced to share power, this could turn easily into anger and nastiness. But as his own boss, he used it more effectively."[15]

By acknowledging this truth, he was able to move past his *Citigroup* failure to a future of great success. In March 2000, Dimon became CEO of *Bank One*, a large Chicago institution that was the result of a merger and had reported a loss of more than $500 million dollars. However, within three years under Dimon's effective leadership, the bank was earning billions in profit and the stock price had risen by 80%.

In an ironic turn of events, Sandy Weill, who had ousted Mr. Dimon from *Citigroup* watched as he became the CEO of a new company when *Bank One* merged with *JP Morgan Chase* and is now one of the most stable financial institutions in the world. He also learned an important lesson about another crucial part of running a large and successful operation; that of succession planning to ensure a capable, competent, and like-minded individual was being prepared for the job.

Toward that end, he promoted two female executives: Jennifer Piepszak and Marianne Lake. Both were capable and experienced candidates, well qualified and positioned to be considered as the *next* CEO of *JP Morgan Chase*. In a recent interview with *Fox Business News* anchor Maria Bartiromo, Dimon said he "is bursting with pride over these two. [Piepszak] has been in the financial function all over the company and she's becoming the new CFO. And like Marianne, she's got character, and talent, and brains, and is trusted by people,"[16]

Willingness to promote the most qualified individuals and share the spotlight and credit with others is one of many reasons why Mr. Dimon is such a highly regarded financial executive and a great example of how the stigma of failure can be overcome by reflection, hard work, and the decision to change. It is also a testament as to why failure should be regarded as a single event and not a permanent situation or identity for the remainder of someone's career or life.

Part Three: James McNerney, Dennis Muilenburg and The Boeing Co.

The *Boeing Company* is a global firm that has held a virtual monopoly on aerospace research, design, manufacturing, and development for decades, with its closest competitor, *Airbus*— also an international concern. *Boeing* manufactures aircraft, satellites, missiles, rockets, communications and weapons systems for both commercial and military use. The United States Department of Defense accounts for roughly one-third of *Boeing's* business. And the DOD accounts for one-fifth *Boeing's* budget. In fact, *Boeing* is an integral part of our national defense and aviation network, though it has suffered from a lack of transparent, appropriate, and suitable leadership for more than a decade.

From 2005 to 2013 the firm was led by James McNerney as CEO and Chairman, who came to *Boeing* from the *3M Company*, which serves such industries as worker safety, health care, and consumer goods. *3M* manufactures and sell adhesives, fire and personal protection equipment, medical products, and other safety and consumer goods.

When he arrived, McNerney took steps to ensure the *Boeing* stock price and cash flow stayed strong. But he did so by eliminating pensions, cutting wages, and moving production. This damaged labor relations, which in turn negatively impacted production.[17] He did not understand the important fact that the defense and aviation industry is fundamentally different from other manufacturing concerns. It is "a capital-intensive business with very high barriers to entry."

Boeing's highly educated and skilled workforce were alienated by the cost cutting strategies. When McNerney retired in 2015, it was said that he "leaves behind a toxic legacy that future leadership will need to deal with."[18]

McNerney executed his succession plan as he transitioned out of *Boeing;* he brought in Dennis Muilenburg, an aerospace engineer, who was President of the Defense, Space and Security Division. He was promoted to President and COO of the company in 2013 and elevated to CEO in 2015.

Muilenburg had three strikes against him when assuming the top leadership role, namely production quality, decreasing profits and disgruntled employees.[19] McNerney came from a strong business background, with his focus on cost containment, profits and stock prices while Muilenburg is a trained aerospace engineer, a Boeing "lifer" having spent much of his time in research, development and engineering. The engineer part of him needed to understand the commercial side of the operation and he needed to do so quickly. As results revealed, he did well initially but was ultimately unable to lead the firm through the turbulent waters of 737MAX crisis, *Starliner f*ailures, and a slowdown of 787 *Dreamliner* production, as well as revenue losses.

Boeing has been in operation for more than one hundred years and it manufactures a variety of narrow and wide-body aircraft, including the 787, 757 and 737 series. It has sold more than 9,000 units of the 737 aircraft in the past fifty years. The 50th anniversary of the 737 was celebrated at the *Museum of Flight* in 2017.[20] The 737MAX is the company's latest rendition of the 737 series, which has been in production since 1967.

The MAX design upgrade was conceived in 2011 under McNerney. It was fast-tracked to production and released to service in 2017 under Muilenburg. This was part of *Boeing's* quick response to intense competition in the narrow-body aircraft sales niche—especially from *Airbus*.[21]

Most airlines use the narrow-body aircraft for short and mid-range flights. These planes are easier to maintain and repair because they are built lower to the ground. They are easier to load and unload and work well at regional airports. With a smaller footprint, it easier to maneuver runways and at airport gates. Most airlines have embraced the 737 series, and it has been a best seller for *Boeing*. *Southwest Airlines* used the MAX as a large part of its fleet, with 34 in service. This greatly impacted their bottom line in 2019; they suffered a 21% profit loss in the fourth quarter.[22]

In an attempt to stay competitive, *Boeing* wagered that using the existing airframe and installing a heavier and more powerful engine would give them a competitive edge. Pilots were already very comfortable with the aircraft, which would not have to be completely reengineered, thus providing substantial savings. The upgraded engine was supposed to provide better performance and not require as much training as a totally new aircraft design, providing yet more savings.

To compensate for the heavier and more powerful engines, *Boeing* designed a software package the *Maneuvering Characteristics Augmentation System* (MCAS). This was a flight-control package that would activate if notified by the flight computer that the nose of the plane was too high. MCAS would override the system and lower the nose so the aircraft did not go into a stall. The MCAS system failed horribly, on October 29, 2018 when Lion Air flight 610 plunged into the Java Sea off the coast of Indonesia, killing all 189 passengers and crew on board.[23]

False data was transmitted from a sensor, which activated the MCAS and sent the Lion Air craft into a nose-dive. The pilots attempted to override the system, to no avail. A year later, on October 25, 2019, a "synopsis of the report, presented in slide-show format to victims' relatives, put the bulk of the blame on Boeing for introducing an automated system in the Max without adequately briefing airlines and their crews about its existence or instructing them how to override the software should it malfunction. It also pointed to maintenance issues on the Lion Air plane."[24]

The same tragedy happened again, four months later, on March 10, 2019, when 157 people perished on Ethiopian Airlines Flight 302. The aircraft went down in a nose-dive crash involving another 737 Max with yet another MCAS system failure. This time, the MAX was grounded in nearly every country in the world.

After the investigations were complete on both crash events, it was determined that some of the flight manuals and training did not contain any information about MCAS. Besides design flaws and inadequate pilot knowledge and training on the system, the National Transportation Safety Committee—Indonesia's version of the United States' National Transportation and Safety Board—"blamed Boeing and the FAA" for not considering "the likelihood of loss of control of the aircraft" if MCAS failed."[25]

The 737MAX had been developed before his tenure and Muilenburg had no input into the decision to redesign the 737 instead of developing a new plane. He inherited that flawed process after many of the major design and engineering decisions had already been made. He made progress to improve the labor relations and was hard at work on the cultural issues that troubled the firm. Then came the two 737 MAX airline crashes and 346 deaths with the ensuing investigations, litigation, fines, and the grounding of over 400 MAX aircraft.

Muilenburg and his senior leadership responded poorly to the public grief and outrage for the loss of life. They did not respond quickly enough to pressure from the board to get the 737MAX recertified by the end of 2019 as originally hoped and intended. Internal emails were leaked showing a culture of arrogance and lack of care and concern about production quality.

Then, the *Starliner* unmanned space craft, developed jointly with NASA, failed to reach the International Space Station in December 2019. The 787 *Dreamliner*, a cash cow for *Boeing*, was facing a production cut from 14 to 12 per month, due to the slowdown in orders, as well as tariff and trade conflicts with China. At that point, with cash hemorrhaging, litigation pending, and so much accumulated failure, the Board decided Muilenburg was unable to restore confidence with shareholder or defense and commercial customers.

It was time for him to depart.

Brittian Ladd, contributor for the *Observer*, wrote about the problem with the 737 Max and the grave errors made by *Boeing* leadership.

> *The 737 Max is a flawed design. Instead of building a new plane to meet the needs of a specific market, Boeing's senior executives, including CEO Dennis Muilenburg, made the decision to upgrade the 737 in an attempt to get the plane to market sooner to prevent its largest competitor, Airbus, from securing orders for its own aircraft. When testing revealed that the heavier engines and the forward placement location of the engines on the 737 Max created new and unsafe flight characteristics,*

did Boeing shut down the program? No. Boeing made the decision to come up with a software fix to force a solution to the fact that the company had pushed the original design of the 737 far past its limit.[26]

Boeing boasted of having a culture of "safety-first," a premise now being questioned by commercial customers, passengers, and flight crews alike. After the *Lion Air* crash, *Boeing* said the MAX was "as safe as any airplane that has ever flown the skies." However, both crashes were confirmed by experts to be the result of a systemic failure in the MCAS software and lack of information in manuals and inadequate pilot training.

Engineers allegedly knew of the problems a year before the first crash.

It came to light October 2019 that Muilenburg had heard about the electronic test pilot warnings from the Chief Technical Pilot, Mark Fortner, who provided input about the flawed system. This warning from the CTP should have prompted *Boeing's* leadership to ground the 737MAX until the problems could be resolved. But the MAX continued in service.

Then came the *second* crash.[27]

On March 10, 2019 *Ethiopian Airlines* Flight 302 went down. Investigators found evidence that the pilots had struggled with the MCAS, which had been activated shortly after takeoff when incorrect information was sent to the flight computer. The nose of the plane was pushed down, and pilots were unable to make corrections, which caused the plane to crash. On March 13, the 737MAX was grounded by the FAA and the aircraft was grounded globally on March 18.

In June of 2019, Brittan Ladd wrote another article calling for Muilenburg to resign, and citing his multiple leadership deficiencies. His credibility became strained, thin, and then non-existent as more details about engineering and software failures came to light, especially in light of his background as an engineer. He resisted calls to resign and promised that the software would be fixed, all safety issues addressed then resolved, and the MAX planes would be recertified by the FAA, by the end of 2019.

Mr. Ladd wrote:

A leader would have made the decision to hire an independent firm to thoroughly investigate Boeing's culture, decision making, manufacturing process, internal communications, effectiveness of the Board of Directors, relationships with suppliers and, of course, testing and safety procedures.

A leader would keep a commitment to make the results of an independent investigation public along with a list of recommendations for correcting issues and permanently preventing any possibility of any future issues like the MCAS fiasco.

A leader would make sure to shake up the Board of Directors with a goal to replace as many board members with individuals from outside of the aviation industry as possible. [28]

Muilenburg addressed some of these point in an interview with *Bloomberg* Aviation Reporter, Guy Johnson, at the *Paris Air Show* on June 17, 2019. He sounded like *he had read Mr. Ladd's opinion piece and paid close attention.*[29]

Boeing quickly invited an independent examination of their entire process, both from governmental regulators, as well as an independent internal audit. They said they intended to make the information totally transparent. *Boeing* looked into everything from their supply chain partners to engineering processes, inserting checks and balances and further safeguards into their systems. The CEO stressed that the firm knew the importance of safety and described how they were correcting the software and enhancing their pilot training.

The only point he did not address in his June comments was the replacement of any members of the Board of Directors.[30] The board has deep ties to Washington DC, where several directors sit on multiple boards, and there is a definite lack of expertise on this board in the area of aerospace and safety issues.[31] There is perplexity regarding some board members such as Nikki Haley, the former governor of South Carolina, and Caroline Kennedy, the daughter of President John F. Kennedy and former ambassador to Japan. They have no formal training in engineering, or technical expertise.

In fact, the board gets only 5.4 points out of a possible 10 according to performance analytics research firm MSCI, which ranks the quality of governance. It is a "weak board dealing with a crisis situation." And Ric Marshall, executive director at MSCI said, "We're looking at an average governance structure."[32]

The board was aware that *Boeing* spent billions of dollars in 2019, lobbying Congress and the FAA to allow them to take on additional responsibilities to "self-certify" certain safety and technical processes. It was believed that the FAA did not have the technical expertise needed to evaluate, assess, and certify the ongoing innovations within the aviation industry. In October 2018, just four weeks before the *Lion Airlines* crash, Congress passed additional provisions that allowed *Boeing* to take on more safety responsibilities.

Essentially they would oversee themselves—with the blessing of the FAA.

House Transportation Committee Chairman Peter DeFazio (D-Oregon) leads a congressional investigation into how the 737 Max was developed and certified by the FAA, or rather by *Boeing* staff members who are supposed to be doing the work of the FAA. DeFazio is worried about *Boeing* and says they may be, "hanging Chief Technical Pilot Forkner out to dry to deflect blame from others within the company. I don't believe he was a lone wolf. I think the pressure started at the top."[33]

DeFazio says evidence already uncovered by his investigative committee points to a "systemic failure" inside *Boeing,* as management ramped up pressure to develop and manufacture the 737 Max *quickly* to maximize profits. "This goes far beyond one individual. This was cultural," he says, adding, "This is what was formerly a company of incredible integrity making great products, and they can get back to that, but they gotta clean house."[34]

A *Yahoo News* article cites a June 2018 email where one employee wrote his own analysis of the problem: "It's systemic. It's culture. It's the fact that we have a senior leadership team that understands very little about the business and yet are driving us to certain objectives," while not "being accountable." Other emails referred to in the article reveal employees knew about the lack of quality and selection of lower cost vendors to promote profits. The attorney representing the Ethiopian crash victim's families, Robert Clifford, is very blunt in his assessment that *Boeing* culture led to "preventable and unnecessary deaths." Other employees question the competence of *Boeing* designers and engineers, with one stating simply, it is a "piss poor design."³⁵

There were more than 100 additional emails released in early 2020 that show how deep the flawed culture and design problems were embedded. In a *Fox News* article, three emails were published as a sample of many others:

> *'This airplane is designed by clowns, who are in turn supervised by monkeys,' one Boeing employee wrote in a 2017 instant message exchange apparently bashing fellow colleagues at the company.*
>
> *'Would you put your family on a Max simulator trained aircraft? I wouldn't,' another employee asked a coworker in a 2018 conversation before the first crash. 'No,' the person responded.*
>
> *I still haven't been forgiven by God for the covering up I did last year, one employee wrote in 2018, referencing interactions with the FAA.*³⁶

There are some five hundred 737 MAX aircraft currently grounded and *American Airlines* and *Southwest Airlines* both extended the time frame for the 737s to remain grounded, from October 2019 until March 2020. In early October 2019,

Qantas Airlines grounded some of their older 737 Next Generation (NG) units due to cracks found in wings of the older models. The *Seattle Times* reported that about fifty planes, or about five percent of the fleet, have been grounded due to cracks in the NG model series of the 737 after "urgent inspections worldwide."

Boeing has additional problems with a rear wiring harness to be fixed, as well as "inspecting more than 400 stored 737 Max jets after discovering tools, rags and other debris left in the fuel tanks of newly built planes."[37] The firm is settling financial claims with *AeroMexico Airlines*, *Southwest*, *American* and will pay a fine of at least $20 million to the FAA. There are civil suits filed by the families of the victims as well as by various other airline firms and associated vendors up and down the supply chain.

On January 9, 2021, Sriwijaya Air Flight 182 plummetted from 10,000 feet and crashed in the Java Sea, just like the Lion Air Flight 610 in October of 2019. The Sriwijaya aircraft was a 27-year-old Boeing 737-500 model, not the 737MAX that has been grounded for over 20 months. The pilots were experienced and the 737-500 model has a good safety record. The airline, started in 2003, has a solid safety record, with no fatal accidents.[38] Nonetheless, the loss of 62 passengers and crew members simply added to the list of problems with

Boeing and will be felt just as keenly as the deaths from the other two crashes involving Boeing aircraft.

The civil litigation will take years.

The *Boeing* debacle (of blatantly ignoring technical and safety issues, downplaying possible defects, and keeping profit as the largest concern, amid fiery crashes and horrific deaths), brings to mind the case of the *Ford Pinto* automobile back in the 1970s. My parents purchased a new *Pinto* station wagon and I proudly drove the shiny new automobile whenever possible. Looking back, it is frightening; there were numerous deaths which occurred when rear end collisions caused fires to erupt and spread very quickly, due to poor designs with the gas tank and placement in the vehicle.

The National Highway Traffic Safety Administration's Office of Defect Investigations found the fuel tank design to be defective. Eventually, 1.5 million *Ford Pintos* and about 30,000 *Mercury Bobcat* sedans and hatchbacks eventually recalled. The Center for Auto Safety played an important role in bringing this information to light, but it took four years for the NHTSA to finally force the *Ford Motor Company* to issue recall notices.[39]

Ford was slow to recall and correct these design flaws and their decisions were initially not challenged until a public outcry after the publication of some outstanding journalistic work by Mark Dowie of *Mother Jones News Magazine*. History shows the worst mistake made *Ford* was how they handled the safety concerns about the rear end collisions and subsequent possibility of fire. *Ford* actually conducted a cost benefit analysis, that when published, came to be known as the infamous "Pinto Memo."

This was a cost-benefit analysis calculating the cost of repairs to the *Pinto* (involving a recall) that would be about $137 million, versus the societal cost of the pain and suffering of burn victims and burn deaths, both to the victims and families, that totaled a mere $50 million. For $87 million dollars ($500 million in 2019, adjusted for inflation), there was a two to three-year delay in fixing the problem, resulting in more deaths. The gist of the memo was published, along with an opinion piece, in *Mother Jones* magazine, claiming 500-900 lives had been lost.[40]

While this was a gross exaggeration of the death toll, the fact that an American firm had actually conducted such a "cost benefit" study outraged the public. Furthermore, several multimillion-dollar settlements were awarded in civil court cases in the years that followed. The safety issues of *the Ford Pinto*, and the way *Ford* executives responded, have long been studied for their ethics value in various case studies at business and technical schools such as the *Illinois Institute of Technology, Center for the Study of Ethics in the Professions, Texas A&M*

University, *Wake Forest* and *Harvard Business School* just to name a few.

At *Boeing*, even if the new leadership can correct company culture, increase quality, fix all the software and safety issues, and have the aircraft recertified by the FAA, the stain on credibility and residue of distrust will remain for many years. While the US governmental authorities may release the MAX737 for manufacture and sale, there may be few or no foreign markets open to *Boeing*. Many countries have grounded the flawed aircraft.

And they show no signs of relenting.

Mr. Muilenburg was dismissed as the CEO on December 23, 2019 and the new leaders say they are determined to restore trust and good will with customers and supply chain partners. The new CEO, Dave Calhoun, was a board member for some ten years—so he was present and had to be familiar with the corporate culture. He was also aware of the propensity to place more importance on shareholder demands, as well as low-cost vendor selection over safety concerns and engineering design quality. He may not be the best person to lead cultural and structural change at *Boeing*. The flawed culture and direct fallout from the 737MAX crashes promises to be yet another business ethics case study that will be reviewed and revisited for years to come.

"Failure is a detour, not a dead-end street."
— Zig Ziglar

"Learning is about failure and recovery from failure."
— Roger Schank

Chapter Ten: Personal Failure and Recovery

Over the past ten years, I have met some courageous and accommodating individuals who have opened up to me, sharing their stories about the different stages of crisis, rescue, and recovery. I have seen them thrive again—beyond their initial losses and failures. Their experiences reveal several strong themes regarding how and why failure happens. These themes include isolation from community, shame, lack of confidence, addiction, shock, and trauma—and how these can affect stability, emotional wellbeing, personal lives, and professional leadership.

Some names have been changed to shield the individual or members of their families. They agreed to share their stories to foster hope and encouragement to those who have loss and failure in their own lives. Each person has emphasized that their belief system—particularly the Christian faith—has been the foundation of their recovery. It is indisputable that failure is an event—sometimes a very sobering, life altering event. But it does not have to be a person's true identity. It is encouraging to see that recovery and redemption can follow all manner of loss, bad fortune, or failure.

Individuals and families alike have been devastated by criminal activity, drug and alcohol addiction, gambling losses, car crashes, and other calamities. The result can be disability, loss of life and employment, financial ruin from medical expenses, divorce, homelessness, and other unfortunate endings. None of us are exempt from death, disease, or pain and suffering caused by the actions of others. There are also choices we intentionally make as we try to self-medicate and seek relief from emotional or physical pain. These may take the form of emotional affairs, sexual infidelity or harassment, alcohol or drug addiction, financial mischief, criminal activity, lying, and gambling.

As I listened to these stories, I learned helpful lessons. I also found joy, better emotional health, as well as renewed desire to take care of myself and be more self-aware. It is liberating when we learn to release ourselves from unrealistic expectations, thus sidestepping emotional landmines.

Listening to others helps us grow and thrive, and it is comforting to know we are not alone.

Tom's Story

Tom was a successful pastor, author, divisional denomination leader, and ministry executive. He eventually became the leader of a global mission ministry, with a staff of some 500 employees and millions of dollars in the annual budget. He is particularly knowledgeable in the areas of leadership health, intentionality, governance, and dealing with issues of organizational strategy. He was a very effective consultant, working with churches and faith-based non-profit organizations.

His books provided practical information and valuable solutions for organizational governance, as well how to deal with personal loss and upheaval. Tom wrote with clarity and eloquence about his own experience with pain and suffering—or as he called it, "the cost of leadership."

As a young leader there were things he did not know about that cost, including lessons learned in the crucible. As an older, more mature, but still vulnerable leader, he realized, "the lessons could not have been learned any other way. Suffering is the cost of leadership and a prerequisite of becoming a great leader who has deep influence. There is no other way." These words were written at a crucial time in his career, when the veneer was polished and refined, but inside, he was isolated, in deep pain, and becoming weaker and vulnerable to temptation. At that time, he was not aware he would be repeating those words in the future.

As an apparently brilliant and sought-after consultant and speaker, Tom was on the road a lot. And, contrary to his public image, he spent painful hours questioning his own professional progress. He lacked self-esteem, particularly in personal and emotional encounters. He felt pressure to live up to the achievements of other family members, and no matter how much he accomplished it was never seemed to be enough. He was obsessed with hurtful memories of trying to please his parents. He constantly fell short of their expectations, and never really received their affirmation or affection.

Tom suffered from bouts of depression and sadness, even as he excelled as an author, speaker, and executive. His ministry work took him far away from home, his wife, family, and church family for extended periods of time. Being isolated from family affection and church community and suffering from loneliness and deep emotional pain drove him to seek relief in self-destructive ways.

Tom did not follow the advice he gave in his books and on his blog. First, he didn't turn to family and friends for encouragement and to seek professional counseling. He also did not hold himself accountable with his peers and the senior leadership of his organization. These missteps made it easy to self-medicate through abuse of alcohol, improper sexual encounters, and other harmful distractions—all in an attempt to quench the pain and sadness of being lonely and depressed.

His behavior was hidden for a while, but eventually he was on the cusp of being discovered. He went to the leaders of the ministry organization and confessed his failure, and he immediately resigned and entered a rehabilitation program. He and his wife were separated, and eventually the family suffered a painful divorce. Tom lost most of his retirement funds and other financial resources. He was in his late 50s and had to start over. Moving several states away, he found a new home and continued to work on his emotional and spiritual recovery.

Tom did some volunteer work, using his consulting skills, and worked part time for a rideshare firm, as well as other temp-type jobs to earn a living and keep busy. He began to attend church regularly and, over time, dealt with personal issues such as shame and guilt. He also began to address family of origin issues and through blunt honesty—mostly with himself—he began to experience emotional health and wellness.

After several years, he met a compatible, committed Christian woman, and they fell in love and married. He has regained self-respect and has a healthy view of his worth and abilities. Tom is happy and hopeful. I checked on him a year after our first interview, and found him doing quite well. He has accepted a consulting position as the senior executive at a large church where there is an on-going pastoral search. He collaborates with several authors, assisting them with writing, editing, and other aspects of the book business.

And he no longer works as a rideshare driver.

I asked Tom about the most important things he has learned, things that have helped him recover and move forward. He told me shame almost always follows failure, and we eventually must deal with it. But we must first take responsibility for the failure itself and understand the contributing factors. We must then seek help to resolve the problems and then determine to work out the solutions, no matter how difficult they may be. This can include sincere apologies, asking for and giving forgiveness, making restitution, and giving ourselves and others the opportunity to experience closure and move forward.

In his own words, Tom has "resolved the past emotional conflicts and problems to the best extent possible at this time." He knows that in his first marriage, for all parties, the relationship ended with emotional wounds and scars, with pain that may never fully be healed. He also accepts that he may never have the close relationships or respect and credibility he formerly enjoyed with his peers and colleagues. But he has taken the initiative to amend, reconcile, and repair relationships and give closure where possible—always with a contrite heart and "olive-branch" spirit.

Tom has sought forgiveness, forgiven others, and himself. He has actively participated in his own release from the guilt of his failures. He is actually reliving some of the lessons he wrote about in his own books and blogs and taking the advice and counsel that he gave to others over the years. He has sought opportunities to use his talents and skills and resumed work on several projects for various business and faith-based organizations. He has refined his purpose in life and some of his goals, with a view toward a healthier, more transparent and accountable lifestyle.

Tom did not lose his competencies, skills, or talents when he made the choices that lead to his moral failure. But he did lose many current and some future opportunities to *use* those skills and talents. He lost credibility with those who employed him, but engaged in a protracted period of rehabilitation, repentance, and spiritual growth. He eventually found there were other employers and organizations who were willing to take a risk and extend him an opportunity to help rebuild credibility.

As we know, credibility is the quality of being trusted and reliable. A moral failure tarnishes that quality and damages or removes the trust of those who believe in us. John Maxwell says that credibility amounts to the currency we spend, and if we lose it, we are *bankrupt*. But, bankruptcy is an event, not an identity. Those who were formerly bankrupt now own houses and are paying mortgages and car loans. Rebuilding credibility is just as possible as repairing a credit rating. But it takes extra time, hard work, and a measure of persuasion.

It does not have to be lost *forever*.

Simon's Story

Simon, a young man in his early 30s, married his childhood sweetheart. They met in their late teens and have been together for nearly 15 years. After graduation, he was ordained and accepted a role as an associate pastor, beginning his work in Christian ministry and as a newlywed husband. He is currently employed by a non-profit organization in an administrative role, well regarded, highly-effective, and popular with his peers.

His is also a story of redemption.

Throughout his life, Simon had dealt with bouts of depression and sadness, even while being a high achiever. He attended a denominational college, where he excelled as a student and earned a degree that enhanced his raw talent, enabling him to speak, write, and teach, with eloquence and excellence.

Pastor Simon had a heart for church planting. After working as an associate pastor for several years, he and his wife ventured out to plant their own new church, with the goodwill, encouragement, and prayerful support of their former church.

Church planting is hard work,. It calls for patience, time, building relationships, and it usually involves—at least at first— –being bi-vocational. Simon and his wife moved some distance away from their first church and they both found jobs in the area, as they worked to make friends and build relationships in the community. This meant very long days.

Being a pastor involves caring for people during the week, as well as preaching on Sunday mornings and gathering together midweek for Wednesday evening services. There are administrative functions, leadership that needs to be developed, and even the challenges that come with finding a place to meet—dealing with leases, electric deposits, and assorted other details.

Simon and his wife come from strong Christian families with high moral and behavioral standards. Drug and alcohol use, smoking cigarettes, premarital sexual activity, and other "sinful" behaviors were frowned upon. Their church attracted military members from a local Naval base, where some units had been deployed for active combat and returned several months later. There was emotional turmoil, and painful memories and residue after being deployed.

These soldiers and sailors did not find it easy to share with outsiders and developed a culture of getting together to socialize, meeting at bars and pubs to eat and drink together. Simon and his wife befriended some of these warriors and began to build trust and respect with them, joining them for social activities, including drinking and socializing at bars.

Simon and his wife willingly participated in these social activities and drank with their new friends. This may have caused them to be conflicted. It was something they knew would not be acceptable to some of their family members. As their new church family began to grow they continued to work at building relationships and ministering to people in times of pain, crises, and turmoil.

They were sincere and eager to help others.

But, in retrospect, there were some red flags. Simon was able to identify several that, if heeded, could have kept them from trouble. Pastors and their families are frequently held to a high moral and behavior standard and they may try to hide problems or difficulties. They want to remain a bright and shining role model for their congregations. Simon and his wife were isolated from their close friends in their former community and had not developed relationships with local peers who could yet be accountability partners. This is a frequent problem for pastors and their families and a sense of isolation and loneliness can occur.

This caring couple also wanted to start a family, but after several years of praying and trying they were unsuccessful. Medical testing revealed some issues. This was a painful discovery and a deep disappointment for them. The additional pressure on their relationship may have contributed to their increased alcohol intake, as they tried to assuage the pain. They both really wanted to have children and hope seemed to be fading.

After some earnest discussion, their hearts turned toward the idea of being a foster family or even adopting. They began the process of qualifying as foster parents, and eventually they accepted some children into their home. These were difficult children with many problems and caring for them was exhausting and stressful. Simon was working very long hours in his jobs, while trying to help with the foster care. He was also fulfilling all the duties associated with being building a church. His wife was also working, and they had challenges, with the children becoming more difficult to take care of, living expenses, vehicle repairs, and money being scarce much of the time.

Drinking was the way they dealt with stress.

Eventually Simon's alcohol intake reached a dangerous level. His wife and others noticed and cautioned him. His pastoral duties and other employment situations became more stressful.

One day, a close friend committed suicide with a gun.

This was the tipping point for Simon. He started to drown in despair. He drank to excess and got behind the wheel of his car, resulting in an accident and arrest for DUI. The stress and humiliation were unbearable. But he continued to drink heavily and had thoughts of taking his own life. One day, his wife found him on a park bench, extremely depressed, and completely intoxicated.

Things quickly turned dark.

The foster children were taken back by the agency, Simon was dismissed from his pastoral role, and he hit rock bottom. He checked into a rehabilitation center. A month later, clean and sober, he and his wife decided to pick up the pieces and start over. They moved back to their hometown and accepted assistance from family members to find a house, employment, as well as a new church home. He completed his court ordered remedies and, with the help of an attorney and many prayers, received a minimal probation sentence and was able to regain driving privileges. Simon worked full-time and part-time for a while to help clear up some court costs and other debt.

Nearly two years later, Simon is clean and sober, working hard each day to help others and make his family proud. He is faithful in church attendance, appears to be growing in maturity, and is in good emotional health. He and his wife are doing well. I checked in with him recently. I found out that

Simon is back in a leadership role and serves as a director in a non-profit ministry.

He has a firm grasp of where he failed and how to avoid isolation from community and retain moral support. Simon regularly shares his story with others to encourage them and help them see how *they* can recover from addiction. He is careful to be accountable to his spouse and several other accountability partners within the church and ministry community. He is thriving and successful in his work and has a bright future for himself and his family.

Family of Origin / Family Systems

There are some similarities in the stories of Tom and Simon. Both men were deeply affected by family-of-origin issues and from the weight and stigma of shame. They were born into and raised in families where there was a strong adherence to certain behavioral standards and religious mores. It was expected and almost demanded that they would maintain a certain code of conduct. Failure to live up to those expectations produced deep disappointment. This is a common theme that affects most of us in one way or another at different times in our lives.

We bring our beliefs—healthy or unhealthy—and emotional baggage into our adult lives and personal and professional relationships. We may or may not have been provided with the tools needed to develop healthy relationships and lives, communicate with others, and resolve conflicts. Our beliefs, habits, and behaviors are shaped by the quality and depth of the care we received in our upbringing and family life. That life was initially created for us by our parents and other significant caregivers in the family unit, also known as the "family-of-origin."

Our "family-of-origin" is the family group, tribe, or unit into which we were born or adopted. Our parents, extended family members, and significant caregivers helped shape our view of humanity, divinity, and society. They deeply influenced what we believe about ourselves, our value, and our purpose. This has long lasting implications.

We may be raised in a warm, loving, nurturing environment or a cold, harsh, impersonal one, or a combination, all which produce different results. Family beliefs and values are passed down from one generation to another, affected by the abundance or lack of emotional stability and maturity of our parents and grandparents and the significant others who cared for us.

When we do not live up to family expectations, or deviate from accepted rituals and beliefs, pressure may be applied to bring the rebel back into the fold and into compliance. This pressure may take the form of withholding of physical affection, verbal affirmation, and approval. It may even be ridicule disguised as teasing. In severe cases, it may escalate to a constant barrage of sharp and comments, or even physical or sexual abuse.

If one parent abuses the children and the other parent is aware but does not intervene, the victim suffers *twice*. They first endure the abuse and then emotional confusion and anguish as to why no one rescued them, especially close family members who were supposed to nurture and protect them. The damage can affect every family member to varying degrees and over many years. In such cases, counseling and therapy can be beneficial, helping to heal the emotional aftermath and bringing reconciliation to family relationships.

Family groups interact and develop deep emotional connections, referred to as family *systems*. Psychiatrist Murray Bowen was an expert in the field of family systems and how they affect individuals and family units. Through decades of research and observation, he developed the *Bowen Family Systems Theory*, a collection of eight concepts about how families and groups interact. The concepts are useful for individual and family therapy. I touch on a few of them below to provide flesh and bones for some content in this chapter.

The *Bowen Family Systems Theory* "views the family as an emotional unit and uses systems thinking to describe the complex interactions in the unit." A system is "a regularly interacting or interdependent group of items forming a unified whole"[1] such as a number system, an ecosystem, or a family system. Systems thinking is "is a multi-layered phenomenon," and it encompasses several themes, one of which is methodology, "defined as a tool, process, and/or model-based approach and that generally assumes that if one is using these tools and techniques then one is 'doing systems thinking' or 'being a systems thinker.'"[2]

Systems thinking is a way of looking at an entire system and seeing how it is put together, what cycles and trends are in place, how the parts or members are interconnected, and how their behavior affects each member, as well as the system as a whole. In family systems, family members are "intensely connected emotionally," which in turn "profoundly affect their members' thoughts, feelings, and actions" to the point that it may seem that family members all have the same "emotional skin."[3] Observing the family or other type of system from this vantage point is a way to see what may be working or not working for the entire group, allowing solutions to be considered and deployed. In the case of the family system, there are unique challenges because the members are human beings and not machines, molecules, or data points.

Within family systems, members are sometimes so interconnected that they "solicit each other's attention, approval, and support and react to each other's needs, expectations, and upsets."[4] These deep connections cause members to be interdependent, and when changes occur in one person, there is a good chance there will be "reciprocal changes in the functioning of others." There are varying levels of interdependence, but it is always there. Even when people try to distance themselves or disconnect from their families, some measure of the interdependence is still present and in effect even when efforts are made to isolate themselves from their family or significant relationships.

Family members who depend upon one another do so for a variety of physical and emotional benefits, such as working together to keep family members safe, and to provide housing, food, transportation, and other physical benefits. There are also positive emotional benefits, such as love and affection, sympathy, a sense of belonging, community, and purpose. Within the emotional component of interdependence, there is the probability that the connection may produce a high level of tension or excitement. Too much tension can lead to increased stress among the members because the resulting anxiety can "escalate by spreading infectiously, leading to a sense of being overwhelmed, isolated and having a loss of control."[5]

At this point, the members who feel most overwhelmed need immediate relief from these intensified feelings and begin to "accommodate the most to reduce tension in others." This reciprocal interaction of accommodation leads to one or several members literally absorbing the anxiety within the family system. It may involve pressure to give up control of independent choices and replace them with the choices of the others they think may be better suited to the happiness or best interests of the family.

Star Trek fans may recall in the movie, *First Contact*, a phenomenon known as the Borg, a massive moving cube of cyborgs that overpowered and assimilated individuals, groups, and technology into their own collective. Assimilation was obviously in the best interests of the collective and was required. "We are the Borg. Lower your shields and surrender your ships. We will add your biological and technological distinctiveness to our own. Your culture will adapt to service us. Resistance is futile."[6] There was no differentiation permitted or tolerated in the hive group of the Borg. Physical changes occurred as "nanoprobes" invaded the blood stream of humans, creating a network that transformed DNA and eventually caused changes to the mental processes, weakening then breaking down their resistance to compel obedience and assimilation.[7]

Pressure from family members can be intense and work much in the same way, by wearing down accommodating family member(s) who become the most vulnerable to emotional problems and addiction issues. It may feel like they are in the grip of the Borg, being absorbed into a collective and their individuality is being stripped away. The tension and anxiety produced may, in turn, lead to mental health disorders, overuse of alcohol, use of illicit drugs, seeking solace outside the family or group in the form of emotional or physical affairs. There can also be symptoms of, or actual physical illness brought on by the intensified long-term stress and anxiety. [8]

There are two types of anxiety, according to research conducted by associates Michael Kerr and Murray Bowen, "Chronic anxiety often strains or exceeds people's ability to adapt to it. Acute anxiety is fed by fear of what is; chronic anxiety is fed by fear of what might be. They go on to say that acute anxiety is generally associated with specific events, chronic anxiety is the result of people's reactions to a disturbance in the balance of a relationship system." All life forms share some measure of anxiety, having this as a common thread, rather an automatic response to stress.[9]

We also can experience anxiety caused by trying to live up to the expectations of our parents and family group, especially if those expectations are unrealistic or based on unfulfilled aspirations other family members had for themselves. Psychologist Adam Grant recently wrote about this on *Twitter*: "We focus too much on trying to live up to others' expectations—and too little on forming and fulfilling our own expectations of ourselves. To separate image from identity, ask what goals you would pursue if no one would ever find out what you achieved."[10]

Bowen advocates working to change the *whole* family system from within, to resolve anxiety and move toward emotional stability and maturity for *all* members. In times of trouble, some people leave the family unit, creating distance and disconnect to alleviate their anxiety, while trying to achieve differentiation. This does not work well and the best results are seen when the one seeking differentiation and resolution of anxiety has "the ability to be in emotional contact with others yet still autonomous in one's own emotional functioning is the essence of the concept of differentiation."[11] In short, this means being your own person, able to think, feel and act in your own individual best interests.

Australian researchers Linda Mackay and Jenny Brown have studied Bowen's research and written extensively about family systems and therapeutic approaches. They believe assisting individuals toward self-differentiation is important and effective in emotional health and for individual and family therapy. They state, "Bowen's cornerstone concept of differentiation of self is defined as the capacity to think, feel and act for self while in connection with important others; and it includes the capacity to integrate both thinking and feelings to assist in self-regulation."[12]

The premise is further supported in research conducted by Rabbi Edwin Friedman, an expert in family therapy and leadership. He is known for expanding the *Bowen Family*

Systems Theory from a clinical context to institutions and religious congregations. In his book *Generation to Generation*, Friedman explains that the position we hold in the family, first son, middle child, etc., is part of our uniqueness and the one thing we never give to anyone or share. It is part of our differentiation, an emotional connection we have within the family group. The positive or negative emotional aspects of the position can slow our progress in life or enrich our development. The more we know and understand about our position and "how to occupy it with grace and savvy, rather than fleeing from it or unwittingly allowing it to program our destiny, the more effectively we can function in any other area of our lives.[13]

Michael Kerr, another family therapy systems expert, concurs with Friedman's research, especially in the area of "leadership through self-differentiation." They both conclude that within families—and also within churches and other organizations—systems develop between interconnected members, with each having its own emotional makeup and individual levels of differentiation. The leader of the group is most effective when he or she is acutely aware of, and primarily concerned with, his or her own differentiation.

When leaders are able to develop their own differentiation, it promotes stable emotional health through self-regulation, where they become a calm and rational presence, while others are anxious and stressed. They hold the vision and values of the organization in the forefront, exercise strong and definitive leadership and develop their teams and senior leadership.[14] A prime example is in the historical account of Jesus.

Jesus as a Self-Differentiated Leader

Dr. Robert Creech, professor of Christian Ministries at *Baylor University*, has constructed a research paper where he discusses the New Testament life of Jesus in light of the Bowen concept of self-differentiation. He proposes that Jesus demonstrates "a high level of differentiation of self" based on experiences recorded in the gospels of the New Testament. Taking "a naïve approach" that the gospel's portrayal of Jesus is reliable and accurate, whether one takes the description of Jesus as a historical or literal interpretation, the level of differentiation is still "a valid subject for study." The highlights of this insightful article are shown in the paragraphs following.

Dr. Creech describes "differentiation of self is a process managed in the context of one's extended and nuclear families as well as a phenomenon placed in our generations." Neither Joseph nor Mary succumbed to shame despite tremendous social pressure during the betrothal period and her pregnancy. Their ability to withstand the societal pressures and rely on their inner feelings and knowledge shows they were differentiated to a large degree.

Iin Luke chapter two there is the account of when Jesus was and was missing for a short time until his anxious parents found him in the Temple. The ensuing eighteen years were spent in the home of Mary and Joseph, though it is believed the latter died before Jesus began his three-year ministry. Jesus became head of the house, taking care of his mother, a responsibility he continued until the last day of his life.

At age thirty, however, he left the household and was baptized and began his ministry. This "might be understood to be a significant act of differentiation from his family of origin" and would have produced much pressure on Jesus and anxiety in the family.

At the same time, his leaving was not a disconnect or an emotional cutoff, but rather a differentiation of self. Jesus interacted with his family, specifically (and tenderly) with his mother until the time of his death. He even made provision for her care with his closest disciple, thus proving his intent to remain connected to his family while "taking care of his Father's business" and carrying out self-differentiation in a variety of ways.

Jesus' well-differentiated self is found in his firm resistance to temptation, commitment to his mission, and insistence upon fully committed followers. He allowed the rich, young ruler to depart and told the grieving son to allow the dead to bury the dead. He responded to each crisis thoughtfully and without anxiety. And, he requires those who will be his disciples to also have a high level of self-differentiation from their own family of origin.[15]

In calm moments, my husband and I have observed that we sometimes "fuel" each other when there is a conflict between us. It is like each of us has a can of gasoline and we take turns dousing each other and throwing matches. His family, all of whom are deeply connected, have a saying, "folks get all spun up" when they fuel each other. It sets emotions all atwitter and affects the entire family. I have reflected on how this happened. Examining the triggers and results of emotional turmoil is an area of self-discovery that, if performed well, leads to increased self-awareness and greater self-care and self-regulation.

Once we are on this road of self-discovery, we can begin self-care by firmly establishing boundaries, exploring individual interests and pursuits, and *taking personal responsibility for our choices and actions and happiness.* I can attest that this is enlightening AND empowering. When there is tension within our family, if we seek first to sooth and address our own anxieties, we can then calmly interact with others. We do not flee and can keep the connections while working toward a healthier relationship.[16]

These concepts can be applied to any given situation where people spend a sufficient amount of time together to develop deep emotional attachments. This is evident in the relationships that grow out of being connected in *community* such as congregations in churches or synagogues or even military or law enforcement units. The death of a member of one of these groups can affect the other members as deeply and forcefully as if it were a child or a spouse. We speak of our fellow church members and Christians as belonging to the community of faith.

Witness the death of a law enforcement officer and how scores of officers from sister agencies attend the funeral, sometimes travelling many hundreds of miles. Often they do not have a personal relationship with the deceased, but being part of the law enforcement *community*, they still feel a profound sense of loss. This may be known to some as *esprit de corps*, defined in *Webster's Dictionary* as "the common spirit existing in the members of a group and inspiring enthusiasm, devotion, and strong regard for the honor of the group."[17]

Defeating Shame

As our friend Tom says, it is time to get beyond the burden of shame, because that is a powerful part of the healing process. Shame, like failure, is not our identity. To achieve good emotional and spiritual health, which in turn helps to support good physical health, we must get beyond shame. Laying down the stigma of shame helps us to engage in healthy personal relationships, function well in the work environment, worship freely in our spiritual life, and move forward in recovery.

Dr. Brene Brown, professor at the *University of Houston's Graduate School of Social Work*, has researched the causes, harm, and effects of shame and vulnerability. She has studied the power of shame and says is the most primitive human emotion. Her research on shame has shown "a very high correlation with problems such as addiction, depression, violence, aggression, bullying, suicide and eating disorders. She has also found guilt is inversely correlated with those things. The ability to hold something we've done or failed to do up against who we want to be is incredibly adaptive. It's uncomfortable, but it's adaptive."

In 2012, Brown gave a *TED Talk* about shame and vulnerability. She says shame speaks first that you "are never good enough" and if you can overcome that, it then asks, "who do you think you are?" Shame is a focus on self, saying "I am bad" while the cousin of shame—guilt—focuses on behavior and says, "I *did* something bad." Consider this: "Guilt: I'm sorry. I made a mistake. Shame: I'm sorry. I am a mistake."[18]

Dr. Brown calls shame an "epidemic in our culture." Shame can fester and grow over time while we keep our secret from others by staying silent. By keeping quiet, Brown says our shame will grow exponentially. "It will creep into every corner and crevice of your life," she says, and the solution is *empathy*. When you talk to a friend about your shame, the secret is broken open and the pain can be healed. "Shame depends on me buying into the belief that I'm alone. Shame cannot survive being spoken," Brown says. "It cannot survive empathy."[19]

Approaching shame from a Biblical perspective, as Tom does (being a believer), he says we either believe what the Bible says about Jesus, or we don't. We either believe in what He did at the Cross, namely, that his sacrificial death paid the debt for our sins that separate us from God, or we don't. It is from that foundation that we can move forward, according to our Christian belief system, undergirded by the Scriptural concepts of new life, forgiveness, redemption, and mercy.

Moving forward starts with the forgiveness of sin. In Psalm 103:12 it says, *"As far as the east is from the west, so far has He removed our transgressions from us."* That gives us a fresh start. God forgives us and does not remember us by our sin, it does not define us nor is "sinner" any longer our identity. We are a "new creature" with a new identity, and he forgives us. This opens the way for self-forgiveness, then seeking forgiveness from others. It is what enables us to leave shame behind and move forward in our spiritual and emotional recovery.

The Bible gives us examples of redemption, such as the Parable of the Prodigal Son and the account of the woman caught in adultery.

When the son left his father's home with his inheritance, he travelled to the distant land, and spent his inheritance on immoral pleasures. He became so destitute he ended up sleeping in a pig pen, but eventually came to his senses and returned to his father's home. When his father saw him from a distance, he rejoiced and prepared a party, a robe, and a warm homecoming. He did not yell at or beat his son, he welcomed him home with open arms—no guilt or shame.

The young man got to start over and rebuild his life with his father and family.

Now we do not know, because the Bible does not speak of what, if any consequences he suffered for his actions. We do not know if he contracted a sexually transmitted disease or fathered children or had gambling debts that his father later had to settle. We don't know about the rest of his life, but we do know that his father did not heap shame upon him. He gave him a fresh start and the opportunity to rebuild his credibility and his life. The young man was not burdened with shame and guilt, but instead shown mercy and showered with love, forgiveness, and encouragement.

In John 8:1-11 we find a story about a woman caught in adultery. The Pharisees brought the woman into the middle of the crowd right in front of Jesus. It was the custom and law to stone to death those caught in adultery. But instead of saying anything, Jesus stooped and wrote in the dust. The Bible does not record what he wrote, but some Bible scholars believe he may have recorded the sins of the woman's accusers in the dust. Or possible he wrote out what the law called for—the stoning of *both* parties.

The Pharisees were trying to trap Jesus, and they continued to demand an answer from him as to how this matter should be handled. Jesus stood and said the first stone should be thrown by the one who had never sinned. He stooped down again and resumed writing while the accusers began to slip away until no accuser was left.

The people who remained, those who had not accused the woman or tried to entrap Jesus, would have observed Jesus ask the woman about her accusers. The New International Version records this short exchange in John 8:10-11, *"Then Jesus stood up again and said to her, 'Where are your accusers? Did even one of them condemn you?' When she replied, she said no and he spoke words of new life and mercy to her, 'Neither do I. Go and sin no more.'"*

The Bible does not record more about her story, she remained anonymous and forgiven. We can only speculate as to what her life was like after her intensely personal encounter with Jesus who, contrary to the feverish demands of the

Pharisees, did not judge and condemn her. I prefer to believe she was able to move forward to develop into a healthy, productive, and well-adjusted person who loved and helped others. I think she remained humble, grateful, and deepened her relationship with God the Father. We know that the emotional and spiritual weight of shame was removed from her at that moment, for that offense.

The powerful truth of shame removed is what we are to remember and act upon in our own journey to recovery.

"We are not a product of what has happened to us in our past. We have the power of choice."
— Stephen Covey

"The veil of self-indulgence was rent from head to foot. I saw my life as a whole."
— Robert Louis Stevenson

Chapter Eleven: Self Discovery is Painful

A Humorous Part of My Story

Life is full of twists and turns. We discover that we are gifted at some things we did not know and not as good at other things we thought we were doing well. Through the process of self-discovery we can evaluate our gifts and skills. While this can be valuable for personal growth, it may also be painful. If practiced on a regular basis, while employing stark honesty, this process can be a profitable exercise, indeed, even a gift. Unfortunately, most of us have a hard time being objective when it comes to examining ourselves. We often view our lives and abilities through the proverbial rose-colored glasses until we get a reality check. With our head reeling and knees wobbling, we begin to ask, "what happened here?" The answers are often unexpected, unpleasant, or unwelcome.

Sometimes all three.

Performing a regular deep-level self-assessment, and checking in with others to receive honest feedback, can protect us from those unexpected surprises. Or at least soften the blow so we are not too badly bruised or damaged. It is preferable to recover from a stumble rather than a fall, or from a bruised ego rather than a fractured one. It is seldom pleasant to discover we are doing something wrong, creating our own problems, or wreaking havoc for others. Improving things often involves changing how we do things and often requires learning new things. This can be difficult, and sometimes we choose to step out of the situation because adapting is bothersome.

An example: I don't like to read instructions about putting things together or fixing something, nor do I purchase extra parts that, in my opinion, should have been included. The process turns me into a very grumpy person—like a porcupine, all bristly and impatient. I'm a plug and play person, and I shouldn't have to pay extra for that. But that's not the only thing that cooks my grits, as we say in the south. My view is that if I buy something it should be fully assembled, with all the parts, ready to go.

Dishwashers and washing machines require "extra" parts such as hoses that were at one time included, and almost any large appliance needs the extra part labelled "electrical plug" that also used to be included. I am *not* a happy camper about this sneaky way to extract more money from my wallet, and I resent the idea that I have to buy a plug for a product that is powered by electricity. I understand that I have to buy gas for a car, but I don't yet have to buy the gas tank for my car (just wait, it will happen!) My porcupine spines are already engaging.

And don't even get me started on the plugs for the latest I-Phone.

My opinion, however, doesn't change reality. Appliances are sold without electrical cords, and if I want the new washer or stove to work, I have to buy one. Of course, the one on the old appliance is not configured like the plug on the new appliance. That would make too much sense and be good for the consumer.

As I fume, chug, and steam, my husband calmly unfolds the instructions for the washer, vacuum cleaner, or whatever we have purchased. He also buys the additional cord, whether he agrees or not.

He reads "the destructions" (that's southern man-speak for instructions) and 85% of the time, puts the item together quickly, correctly, and uses most of the parts. The other 15%

of the time there is some mild grumbling, undertones of grousing, and a few loud noises as he wields the hammer or drill, but it all comes together in the end. He probably could have made a living back in the day as the owner/operator of a fix it shop in some small town, like Emmett on *The Andy Griffith Show*. But I would have lasted only a couple days before throwing a vaccum cleaner or coffee pot out the front door.

Let's talk about choices. I can choose to keep my rigid and outdated opinion, as well as my childish operating procedure--or I can adapt. I could choose to wear dirty clothes, or wash them in the creek by beating them on a rock, or even go to the laundromat. Better yet, I could purchase a new washing machine, with the proper hoses and electrical cord and have the convenience of a home laundry system.

It is entirely my choice—well, at least regarding *my* clothes. My husband is going to make sure his clothes are washed in a proper washing machine and dried in an electrical dryer with the proper cord attached.

Self-discovery reveals there are a few things I can do spectacularly well, a few things I can do very well, many more things I can do at an adequate level, and then there are some things that I should entirely avoid. I have removed a stove from the kitchen, taken the old cord off, put it on the new stove and hooked it up. It worked well, but it was absolutely necessary for me to sit down with the instructions (by myself, in a well-insulated room) and read them. Oddly enough, I've learned that if I (choice) take the time to (change) read the instructions, assemble the right tools, refer to the instructions frequently, it seems to work out. I just don't necessarily want to change my methodology, and it's a humorous (to others) but painful (for me) process.

As human beings, we all have some tradition or process in our lives that we stubbornly cling to, even when change would yield better results, lower blood pressure, and happier family time. Our "thing" might be a personal pet peeve, a comfortable way of handling work situations, reluctance to change long held beliefs or methods, or just plain pride or stubbornness. Adopting change is an opportunity to learn and grow personally, to gain wisdom and knowledge, to improve our interactions with others, as well as inanimate objects such as clocks, fans, and stoves. It's our choice. There are many reasons we avoid or procrastinate about change, but life marches forward.

I doubt any company will seriously consider my opinions about hoses and cords.

Carl's Story

This next story was shared by Carl, who experienced depression and distress in leadership as a result of failing to change, even after identifying areas that needed improvement and correction. He grew up on a farm in a family with a strong work ethic, clear values, and deep Christian roots—roots ingrained for generations. They had a good home, plenty to eat, most of their needs and wants satisfied, and a consistent schedule of chores, school and church attendance, and related social activities.

When Carl was a teenager, his younger brother died in a tragic accident on the farm. This traumatic event affected the entire family, and Carl began to experience deep sadness and depression. Somehow, he felt guilty about the accident. These negative emotions haunted him during his teen years and well into adulthood.

After he graduated from high school, Carl continued to work on the farm, and in the community, as well. He took on some leadership roles in his church as a Sunday School teacher and youth group leader, and he was appointed chairman of a local church organization. As he served in various capacities, he felt called to become a pastor. He moved to another state and pursued a Bible college degree to prepare for the ministry. After he started his studies, Carl found a part-time position and a new church home.

He settled in nicely.

Carl was assigned an internship and worked though it successfully while assuming leadership roles at his new church.

Again, he taught Sunday School, served as a deacon, music leader, and worked with the youth group. Soon, he met his future wife and within a short time, was a happily college graduate. He helped the pastor and served the congregation by preaching and teaching, whenever possible. He was well received and loved by the church members. And when the pastor retired, the church members called Carl to lead them.

After he and his wife prayed, he accepted the position.

For the first few years, the church flourished, gaining new members and almost doubling in size. Carl was an effective pastor, gifted in preaching, teaching, and discipling new members. He worked hard with the children's programs and ministry because there were only a few families with children attending the church. He was somewhat concerned that the census of children remained low—not a good sign for a growing church.

There were continuing challenges with some of the church programs, and it was difficult to find and retain leaders. Changes had occurred over the course of 2-3 years. Attendance was not as regular as originally thought. Families had pressing work obligations, social events, and children's school activities. The constant tug of technology, social media, and other busyness kept some families more fully engaged than was the case decades earlier. More and more, it was a challenge to get enough people to volunteer for workdays, perform maintenance, attend meetings, or even fill necessary positions for teachers and nursery and music ministries.

Pastor Carl performed the majority of ministry work such as hospital visitations, evangelistic outreach, and chaplaincy care for the home bound. He was a caring shepherd who worked diligently, even taking church members to the doctor and other such tasks. He attempted to fulfill scriptural instructions to "equip the saints" to do some of the ministry work of the church, but it was difficult to find people willing to be trained.

Ultimately, there was a succession of deaths within the church, some of whom were considered part of the backbone of the congregation. Pillars of the church. It was painful and lonely as he conducted funeral after funeral of friends and loved ones as his church family grieved deeply. Some of the elderly who died had been part of the fabric of the congregation for decades. On a personal level, Carl was struggling to find ways to comfort and encourage his congregation, while continuing to experience sadness, isolation, and depression of his own.

On two separate occasions, he and his family sought to leave the church to become missionaries. They believed perhaps that was a new direction and call on their family, but both times it did not work out. Problems arose with extended family, personal health concerns, and other factors that played into their decision to abandon the pursuit of a mission assignment. He had presented a plan to the church where he would step aside within a certain time frame, believing they would be sent out to the mission field, but that did not come to pass. At that point, he retained the pastoral role but "felt as though he had used up a lot of his leadership capital."

The congregation had always been very kind, generous, and full of brotherly love and good will, caring deeply for and about each other. The members were prayerful, steadfast, and mature, with clean hearts and lives. Their devotion to the church and to God was sincere and deep and their support and respect for their pastor was evident. Activities and events continued, such as Vacation Bible School, banquets, and ministry events that brought great joy. There were even a few good successes such as training several new Sunday School teachers and developing some new deacons.

Even so, the human factor came into play, and there were undercurrents of strife, discontent, and a lack of growth plagued the church. In the years that followed Carl's attempts to pursue the mission field, there were few new members and the church dwindled in size and strength. There were some personality conflicts and leadership tussles, and administrative chores that were completed late—or not at all. Carl pursued additional ministerial education and tried to develop skills and identify areas where he was not particularly gifted or strong.

But even this did not translate into the kind of effective results he desired, or the church needed.

Carl finally conducted a painful evaluation of his talents and the poor results of his leadership within the church, and in the process, he looked honestly at his strengths and weaknesses. He admitted that he lacked certain leadership skills and did not use good practices in administrative management and conflict resolution. He was unable to resolve certain personality conflicts among members even after several valiant efforts. It was difficult for him to delegate or follow up on assignments he had given to others. He was authorized by the deacons to hire an assistant to perform some of the routine administrative tasks and contact with church members, but for whatever reason, he did not take advantage of this opportunity. Carl was a faithful steward of the church finances and resources and this played into his reluctance to hire someone to assist him. This did not work out well for him as he continued to be overwhelmed with management and administration details.

As a last resort, he sought assistance from an experienced and skilled mentor and reluctantly agreed to try some new things. Carl described his vision for the future of the church and what he had on his "wish list" for development. He was given a list of recommendations for improving his situation and expanding his skillset and some exercises to complete. After a few months, he determined that he did not think he could/or did not want to adapt to the changes he needed to make, on both a personal basis and within church structure.

When Carl was agonizing over what he believed was solely a lack of leadership ability and competency on his part, he did not fully consider the implications of the ongoing and problematic cultural makeup of the congregation. He knew there was a problem. He would have to remove and reassign several people who were involved in current leadership and bring others on board. A daunting task. He would also have to resolve some long-standing challenges to change congregational culture.

There were several individuals and families that had been in the church for decades. Their reluctance to adapt to almost any change was a major impediment to growth. These people were wary of new methods or programs, even if they would truly benefit the church. They believed there were many traditions and methods that, if changed, would weaken or dilute the doctrines held by the denomination and violate "how it was always done."

They did not realize, and Carl could not effectively clarify for them, that he did not wish to change theology or disrupt doctrine. They just needed to stop doing the things that were not working, and try some new things to improve some of the basic operations of the church. For many years, procedures were so bound up, it could literally take months to make simple changes or decisions about things such as installing handles on a cabinet or changing the paint color on a door. It was difficult to have consistency in mundane things like making sure the trash was put out on a regular basis or that the trash bill was actually paid.

The deacon board made almost all decisions on acquisitions and expenditures. This included things that were totally out of their purview and experience, such as what type of vacuum cleaner or mop and bucket the cleaning staff should be allowed to have and use. Challenges to this way of doing things were not well-received. It was another case of being stuck in tradition of how "things were always done." Not only was this an unintentional slight on the part of the deacons, but they caused hardship for the cleaning staff by not acknowledging their expertise and letting them pick the proper tools and equipment needed to do their job.

The person who performs the work should, within reason, be able to request and receive the tools and materials needed to do their best work. It should be noted here that staff members sometimes do not have the extra funds to purchase supplies and equipment and turn in receipts. It creates great hardship and tension for them personally and distresses their family and financial budget. For accountability and oversight, it is better to work out a way for the staff to make purchases without involving their own money. This is just one example of how good intentions involving stringent accountability and oversight can lead to distress for those not in leadership positions, but who are still valued members of the staff.

Where such tight control by a few individuals and/or families exists, it creates conflict and tension within any church or organization. There is also the dilemma of having rigid controls influenced and guided by a matriarch or patriarch of a church—individuals who have been church members and leaders for a very long time. They have deep connections and understanding of the church and usually have the respect and loyalty of the congregation.

In many ways, the congregation is like a tribe, with patriarchal and matriarchal leaders. Many times, these individuals or families are decision makers and influence the congregation toward their desired preferences about music, worship, lesson plans, celebrations, events, and so forth. They do not take kindly to change—or conflict—and do everything within their power to keep the reins of control firmly within their grasp.[1]

In this scenario, the church congregation really just wants the pastor to be a *chaplain*, someone nearby to provide pastoral care and comfort, lead worship, and preach. But they do not want him to be the actual leader of the church. Those details, it is assumed, are to be handled by the dominant patriarch/matriarch group. This deprives the pastor of a rightful leadership role in the church. In the case of the patriarchs, most would be part of the deacon or elder board. As for the matriarchs, they would likely head up various committees and ministries.

Then there is the threat of manipulation, perhaps by withholding funds, time, or talent, such as when there aren't a sufficient number of leaders for a favored group or ministry. Those who lead can be overly sensitive, annoyed and create conflict if they are challenged or corrected. They will hint that if they do not lead, no one will. They might threaten a favored program or ministry as a manipulative and petty ploy. Those who refuse to lead a program because of a perceived offense or slight are bitter and vengeful. In some cases, the programs are better undone than to be led by such poisonous people. The ripple effect from this kind of church dysfunction is, of course, harmful. Children's ministries left undone will lead to families leaving the church to seek places that will provide ministry for their children. The same is true with singles ministries, programs devoted to the seniors, or other specialty groups in the congregation.

Pastor Carl knew that to challenging the culture of the church leadership would be a long-term undertaking. He was already weary, discouraged, and feeling like he was failing the church family—and his own family. It was at that point he decided to seek employment outside the church, finding a position suited to his skills.

Before he left the church, he arranged for a strong leader to become chairman of the deacons and gave the board some final advice and encouragement. He also stayed in touch and prayed, answering questions when needed and giving encouragement from a distance. Carl's family enjoyed still having a connection with the church family they had known and loved for twelve years.

I followed up with Carl some eighteen months after he left the church. He reported that he tried several positions with different employers before he found his current job as a middle school teacher in a Christian School. Within the church, he was an excellent Bible teacher, effective and comfortable in that role, adept at balancing truth, humor, and practical lessons for life. He was using his skills and competencies to the best advantage in an educational environment in a familiar Christian setting.

There was some "unexpected uncertainty" for him and his family during the job search for Carl and his wife. She started work in the public-school system again. While searching for employment, he remembered being challenged to trust the Lord for his needs and not be anxious. The family had to work through some tight financial situations with vehicles that needed to be repaired and there were weeks when they had very little income. This was an opportunity to build and strengthen their faith as the job and financial situations resolved favorably over time.

He was grateful for his current employment and doing well in all aspects of his personal and family life. Although Carl believes he might enjoy being a pastor again at some point in the future, for now he is content. He and his family are enjoying their time together and life seems simpler now that he has a regular schedule and paycheck with less demands on his time.

During our interview Carl expressed how he was particularly delighted to observe a "highly functional church" works. In the church his family attends, he gets to see firsthand the deep levels of coverage from professionals within the congregation to handle administrative and committee roles. The senior pastor is aware of his own area of strengths and where he needs assistance, and he has invited the associate pastors to handle the areas where he is not gifted or the best person to perform specific tasks. Carl is observing and learning, and he is sure this will be very helpful to him in the future.

As many other leaders before him, Carl has gone through a crucible of pain and self-discovery. He has emerged stronger and healthier after taking a "mental break" and sabbatical time. Personal refreshment is important and sometimes necessary. Temporarily stepping away from a role we love can be wise, allowing us to change our perspective for the better. Carl realized this, and he is now looking forward to the time when he might resume a pastoral or other ministry.

He has learned more about church structure, governance and how a church should operate. He has identified several areas where he will invite assistance from an associate pastor and/or lay leader within the congregation if he ever takes on the pastoral role again.

As he continues to observe and learn, he is also developing strategies to improve in three specific areas of time management and scheduling. He believes this will be of great help to him in the future, as he gains knowledge to equip and prepare him to be a better pastor and church leader. He is adapting and practicing a more balanced approach to his work-life situation.

He feels much better, with a renewed spirit to serve his family and brethren.

"Peace isn't the absence of pain; it is the presence of God in the midst of life's troubles."
— Tony Evans

"Forgiveness is the gift we give ourselves that allows us to get on with our lives instead of being trapped in the past by resentment."
— Rick Warren

Chapter Twelve: Loss and Recovery

Liam's Story

Liam was grew up on a farm in a hard-working family. He and his siblings did their daily chores before and after school. This early experience helped him develop a strong great work ethic and the ability to be part of a team. He looked to one of his older brothers as a lifelong mentor, and he had a healthy and loving relationship with his entire family. After attending college, where he studied business management, Liam accepted a position at a nearby college, serving in the Financial Department. He spent two years there.

He then travelled to California and studied sales, marketing, organization and management through on the job training, in various roles with different employers. He married his high school sweetheart, and they started a family together, becoming the parents of two healthy, well-adjusted, and good natured children.

Liam was intelligent and skilled at business management and systems. He travelled quite a bit for his employer, but also had interesting personal projects that kept him happy and busy. He was an excellent provider for his family, and they had a very comfortable—even affluent—lifestyle. The children were healthy, his job and marriage seemed good and life was generally going well.

Until it fell apart.

His wife became lonely and depressed. She felt he was absent too much of the time. And unknown to Liam, she succumbed to loneliness and began having an affair. When she finally revealed this, she told him that she no longer loved him. Shock, grief, anger, and many difficult conversations, gave way to a painful divorce.

The family was disrupted, the children's lives were shattered, and Liam was swallowed up by anger and sadness. He described it as a time of realization. He had not been a good husband, having been absent so often. He was devastated and vacillated between hate and anguish, existing in an emotional fog, unable to eat or sleep or perform effectively at work.

Liam was a very new Christian, having received and accepted the gospel message of salvation in middle age. It was a very confusing and difficult scenario, trying to behave as a Christian—kind and amicable—instead of being angry. But he still moved forward and took care of his children, while taking steps to build a new life.

One of Liam's co-workers was a strong and mature Christian, a Sunday School teacher and wonderful friend and example to him. He observed that Liam was emotionally distraught, physically run down, and sometimes ill, even missing work occasionally. One day this co-worker asked Liam, "Have you forgiven her?" He said, "she doesn't have to ask for forgiveness. Forgiveness comes from you!" That was such a powerful question and enlightening statement that when Liam considered it he had what he described as "almost instant peace."

It took time, prayer, and adjustment, but he began to feel better physically. He gained emotional strength and started eating and sleeping better. Once again, he could concentrate at work, make better decisions and good progress with the basic details and demands of life. He also started to understand more about Scriptural precepts and what it meant to live as a Christian—even in painful and difficult circumstances.

After a short time, he was able to speak with his ex-wife more amicably. He was eventually able to ask her if she had forgiven herself and was able to guide her to some of the same spiritual truths he had learned. As more time passed, Liam met and married a lovely Christian lady. They raised three children and were active in church—even taking missionary trips. Liam's ex-wife also became a Christian and married a wonderful man. The extended family is congenial, friendly, and has occasional gatherings with each other and the children and grandchildren.

Liam was blessed in his work and thrived in his career. After spending some 30 years in the risk management industry, he retired. His final role was serving as an executive member of the senior leadership team and as an officer in a major corporation. He and his wife are still active in their church, and he serves as a committee member and team leader for various ministries. One of his greatest delights is mentoring at-risk and underprivileged youth, and he is a strong advocate of education.

> *"Forgiveness is the gift we give ourselves that allows us to get on with our lives instead of being trapped in the past by resentment."*
> — Rick Warren

The Fruit of Forgiveness

Liam's life was changed when one man used his words to urge him to consider *forgiveness*. This kickstarted recovery through the fog and pain of divorce and helped with repairing relationships. It was the "lollipop moment" that Drew Dudley talks about, but it occurred when one person inspired another to positive action. The result was that an angry man was calmed and nurtured back to health. He went on to influence many other people in business and ministry. The power of this lollipop moment was magnified by the application of forgiveness, which is a choice, a process, as well as a mechanism for healing.

Forgiveness is an intentional decision to let go of bitterness, anger, and hate in order to make room for positive things such as peace, kindness, and moving forward to fully live again. When Liam deliberately chose to apply forgiveness to the mortally wounded relationship with his ex-wife, it opened up the possibility of a measure of peace, as much as was possible between estranged family members and significant others. Family ties were re-connected and emotional wounds were mended. His family has benefited in many ways from the fruits of forgiveness, seen in improved physical and emotional health, the return to meaningful work, and sincere affection between members.

A great definition of forgiveness is found in a white paper published by the *American Psychological Association* for the 59th Annual NGO/DPI United Nations Midday Conference. The definition is from an unpublished PhD thesis written by Mr. C. Philpott, a doctoral student from the *University of Queensland*, Brisbane, Australia. He studied and examined various literature and viewpoints on the subject, then developed his own definition of forgiveness:

> *Forgiveness is a process (or the result of a process) that involves a change in emotion and attitude regarding an offender. Most scholars view this an intentional and voluntary process, driven by a deliberate decision to forgive. This process results in decreased motivation to retaliate or maintain estrangement from an offender despite their actions, and requires letting go of negative emotions toward the offender.[1]*

Medical evidence supports the positive emotional benefits and wellbeing that flow from practicing forgiveness. "There is an enormous physical burden to being hurt and disappointed," says Karen Swartz, M.D., director of the Mood Disorders Adult Consultation Clinic at *The Johns Hopkins Hospital*. Holding anger long term can change your heart rate, increase blood pressure, and damage your immune system. This can, in turn, lead to emotional and physical conditions such as depression, as well as cardiac issues.

Choosing to release anger through forgiveness is soothing and diminishes stress.

Dr. Swartz says forgiveness is "an active process in which you make a conscious decision to let go of negative feelings, whether the person deserves it or not. As negativity is released, "you begin to feel empathy, compassion, and sometimes even affection for the person who wronged you."[2] Swartz and Philpott agree that forgiveness is a deliberate choice that produces positive benefits.

In a 1997 study titled, *Forgiveness: More than a Therapeutic Technique*, Katheryn Rhoads Meek and Mark McMinn sought to "evaluate the current trends in the psychological literature on forgiveness in light of Christian theology and to discuss the resulting therapeutic implications." They concluded, "forgiveness is a powerful therapeutic tool that has a capacity to affect emotional well-being in people's lives when utilized in its proper context." They went on to say that, "it is more than a technique," having a theological and historical context which endows it with healing power. A therapist educated about these bases of forgiveness can "use it effectively with his or her religious and non-religious clients by becoming a therapist who models forgiveness, recognizes fallibility in the client without being condemning, presents choices and consequences around the option to forgive or remain angry, and provides a safe and trusting environment."[3]

According to Dr. McMinn, professor of psychology at *George Fox University*, assisting clients in the process of forgiveness is quite beneficial and helps them accomplish a range of psychotherapeutic goals. These clients often have spiritual values that need to be considered in their psychotherapy. It is helpful to them if they can find "some sense of peace, of releasing the anger, of wishing an offender well instead of harm" and move forward with life. "There have been over 1,000 empirical studies now on the effects of forgiveness in psychotherapy…the empirical data has been so strong, showing that it can help people find a sense of peace in their life that we simply can't ignore it."[4]

There is some difference between how psychologists and Christian theologians might employ the forgiveness process in therapeutic settings. Forgiveness in psychology may be viewed as an intrapersonal, "unilateral act of mercy offered to the offender by the forgiver," where mercy is willingly chosen by the victim. This enables them to release pain and negative feelings, pursue healing, and move forward with their own lives. Reconciliation is not required, although if repentance and remorse are shown by the offender, it may then be considered by the victim.[5]

In the view of Christian theologians and counselors, forgiveness and reconciliation go hand in hand because "God forgives humanity for the explicit purpose of reconciliation" with Him. Sin has broken the relationship between man and God and is only restored through forgiveness. The process is designed to be an interpersonal process between the persons of God and individuals.[6]

In a blog post several years ago, Texas megachurch pastor Tony Evans described the journey very well. He wrote, "Forgiveness is not pretending like it didn't happen or like it didn't hurt. That's called lying. Forgiveness is a decision to release a debt regardless of how you feel."[7]

"Courage is not limited to the battlefield or the Indianapolis 500 or bravely catching a thief in your house. The real tests of courage are much quieter. They are the inner tests, like remaining faithful when nobody's looking, like enduring pain when the room is empty, like standing alone when you're misunderstood."
— Charles Swindoll

Chapter Thirteen: Leading with Integrity

Honoring our Leaders: Vice President Mike Pence

"To those who wreaked havoc in our Capitol today, you did not win. Violence never wins. Freedom wins. And this is still the people's house."
— *Vice President Mike Pence*

Ernest Hemingway coined the phrase "grace under pressure," to describe how a person remains cool, calm, and collected in tense and difficult circumstances. Leaders often find themselves in awkward and uncomfortable situations that can be difficult to resolve. The way they respond, the words they use, and even the tone of their voice or "body language," can be judged. The more visible or public the leader, the more intensely they will be scrutinized, analyzed, and criticized.

One person who is highly visible, constantly scrutinized, and frequently criticized is Vice President Mike Pence. He attends many of the public events where President Trump speaks, and after the fact he must hear and see the many derogatory news reports about his "boss." Nevertheless, Mr. Pence has adhered to a firm policy of supporting the President. Period. He uses phrases such as "…it's an honor to be serving with" and "the privilege of being Vice President."

He is a great and gracious leader and performs well under extremely difficult and often trying circumstances. Many in the government and news media organizations have called President Trump unsavory and disrespectful names and used vindictive and loathsome words to describe him. The President often responds in a way that must be very awkward for our Vice President.

John Maxwell recommends several strategies to use to smooth the way when you are working for a leader who is perceived to be unpopular or difficult. Mr. Maxwell says great leaders seek to build consensus, not lead coup d'états. Leaders keep a check on their emotions and behavior and exercise self-restraint. It is important to find common ground, keep open communication and be positive. Being consistently and intentionally pleasant and courteous is very helpful. So is working hard every day to solve problems for the leader. Vice President Pence is always cordial and strongly supportive and finds positive ways to speak about, and work with the President, which is also one of strategies recommended by Maxwell.[1]

During the 2016 campaign, ugly rumors abounded about candidate Trump, including the embarrassing *Access Hollywood* tape. But Mr. Pence remained firm in his support of Mr. Trump. The Special Counsel investigation into the Russia-gate events, the Biden-Ukraine situation, and other difficult crises have not weakened his support for or loyalty to the President.[2] He always found tactful and gracious ways to support and honor the President, while upholding the best interest of the United States.

Pence is a humble man, who often does things quietly and behind the scenes to encourage others. He took the time to personally call a hospital patient in Rome, Georgia, who was battling infection with the coronavirus. Clay Bentley is an avid Christian and was surprised and delighted to receive the call from the Vice President. Clay shared his story in a *Facebook* post: "So you know you're living in a great country when the Vice President calls you to tell you that he is personally praying for your recovery. Mike Pence, you sir are such a great leader...and sharing the Love of Jesus with you was an honor!!!"[3] No one would have known what the Vice President did, except Clay, had he not shared his story.

In a speech to students at the *National Student Leadership Conference* in Chicago in 2017, Vice President Pence said leaders must be humble and exercise self- control. "They must listen, be humble, have a character people respect, work to serve others and learn from other leaders." Pence also advised that they should "respect those who have been placed above you. Honor them. Learn from them. Follow their example. Give them the honor that they are due," he added. He further advised them, as aspiring leaders to "practice discipline and to practice self-control to become the kind of woman and man that people will respect, and people will follow."[4] Mr. Pence has clearly followed his own excellent leadership advice.

In the days and weeks following the 2020 election, our Vice President was in a no-win scenario, battered from all sides and under extreme and hostile pressure. When the US Capitol was breached, there were individuals calling for his death by lynching. Through it all, Vice President Pence maintained self-control and personal integrity, moved with courage, spoke with calm civility, and acted with resolute dedication to the United States of America. He had to walk through the fiery crucible of the most challenging and severe tests of leadership in his life.

Vice President Pence has emerged refined, with honor and the enduring respect and gratitude of many in our country.

The Difficult Task: Cheryl R.

For some forty years, Cheryl was employed with a global technology firm, working in various roles as a team member, project manager, and administrative leader. At one time, she led several departments, overseeing the work of 300 employees. She took leaves of absence several times to have children. Cheryl enjoyed her work, the various projects, and mentoring, receiving multiple promotions during a long and rewarding career.

I asked her what advice she had for other female employees and leaders who wanted to advance their career. Her advice was to work very hard, take on tasks no one else wanted and do them very well, solve problems for the leaders, carry out their instructions, and make him or her look good. She also said to keep pressing forward, advocate for yourself, and serve the organization with excellence.

Cheryl faced several challenges in her career, some that were quite difficult. She was surprised and chagrined when she was tasked with dismissing two of her top staff members. She knew they were competent, driven, and dedicated team players, and that they were top performers. She did not concur with the decision to dismiss them and decided it was a matter of personal principle that she seek to reverse the directive.

After trying on her own to obtain a reversal, to no avail, she still felt strongly about it and enlisted several other leaders and executives who sympathized. They presented compelling evidence about the talent, competence, and stellar performance of the employees in question, and worked together on the appeal. In her own words, she "fought hard to prevent the dismissals." Despite all their efforts, the appeal was denied. Cheryl knew she had done everything possible, so she reluctantly dismissed the employees, "because it was her obligation to do so."

Thus, she served the organization with dignity and professionalism.

Cheryl says that if we accept a leadership position, we must accept the responsibilities that go with it. Some are pleasant; others are not. In fact, we are sometimes asked to do things we do not like or with which we personally agree. She wanted to serve the best interests of the organization, and obviously one of the leaders above her believed the employee dismissal was in the best interest of the organization. Cheryl disagreed, but she maintained her professional demeanor and carried out her job duties despite her personal feelings. She performed a difficult task in a compassionate manner, with her integrity and self-respect intact, and by practicing the highest level of ethical leadership.

"Memories influence every action and pattern of action you undertake."
— Dr. Daniel Amen

Chapter Fourteen: The Riddle of Experience v Memory

A Gift and A Blessing

This is a book about leadership and how it starts *inside*. Humans have the capacity for light and dark, love and hate, despair and delight. How we respond to the joys and disappointments of life help shape us individually and influence how we lead others. From that vantage point, please consider this last chapter as a gift, a tool, and a blessing. I stumbled upon this information while I was working on this book. It turned out to be some of the most beneficial information I've ever discovered—even life-changing—and it merits careful and thoughtful consideration.

Take your time.

If it helps, you are blessed, and if it does not, perhaps it is a tool for the future or to pass along to someone else. At most, it begs an additional ten minutes of your time that may yield many benefits and blessings.

Daniel Kahneman, psychologist and economist, presented a *TED talk* in Long Beach, California in 2010, where he spoke about the subject of *happiness*. "We are reluctant to admit to the complexity of the definition of happiness. Happy is applied to too many things these days." All of us want to be happy yet, "lay people and scholars alike fall into several cognitive traps that affect how we apply happiness to our individual lives." Most humans want to be happy. We work and strive to find happiness and prefer to be happy rather than sad or distraught. We are responsible for our own life and pursuit of happiness. Helpful information and useful tools can be used in our quest for the happiness part of the life, liberty and the pursuit of, mantra from the Declaration of Independence.

We all have events in our lives that we may describe as epiphanies or game changers. Events so significant that they can help us change our lives. After hearing this *TED talk* for the first time, I wasn't entirely sure how it would help me, but I KNEW, intuitively, it would. Certain words and phrases resonated and registered in my conscious. It's like finding a great shirt that will go with clothing items you already have in your closet. You just know it's a great shirt, so you take it home, pair it with different items and fold it into your wardrobe. It enhances your appearance, and you just feel good wearing it.

Dr. Kahneman started by stating there is confusion between experience and memory, about being happy *in* your life, and being happy *about* your life. They are two very different concepts, but both are "both lumped into the notion of happiness." The big difference is the conflict between "our *remembering* self and our *experiencing* self." We also wrestle with "the idea of "focusing illusion" where we cannot think about any circumstance that affects well-being without distorting the importance of it."

He gave the simple example of listening to a recording of beautiful classical music for 20 minutes. After savoring it until almost the very end, suddenly, there is a flaw in the recording that makes a horrible, jarring, screeching noise. We could say the screeching noise "ruined the whole experience," but it did not. You enjoyed nearly 20 minutes of the *experience* of listening to beautiful music. The screech ruined the *memory of the experience*. After the experience, you are left with a memory, which is ruined, and it is all you got to keep from the experience.

There were the nineteen-and-a half-minutes where the experiencing self, who lives in the present, enjoyed the listening experience. There is the remembering self, which lives in the past and has a damaged memory of the experience because of the horrible jarring screech at the end. But I have found there is a way to live happily with the damaged memory of the experience.

Let me explain.

My husband and I bought tickets for a Valentine's Day Concert featuring Andrea Bocelli. I looked forward to the concert with great anticipation, and on the appointed day, we drove to the downtown area where the event was being held. All went well until we were one block away from the parking garage. Traffic stood still, and time marched on. I got very grumpy and anxious that we would be late. All of the entrances to the garage were blocked off except one and there were hundreds of cars trying to get into it. Some drivers were cutting in line, and others were blocking lanes. It was a mess and the police seemed to ignore all of it, while accommodating the patrons who were walking to the venue.

I felt so irritated I just wanted to go home, but we could not get out of the lane of traffic to get back to the Interstate. Eventually, we were able to get through all of the messy traffic and park the car. It was a short walk to where another crowd was waiting to go through the metal detectors. Almost two hours after leaving home, we finally got to our seats. My husband was slightly irritated.

I was like a tea pot on high boil.

When Mr. Bocelli came out on the stage and started to sing, it was clear I had two choices. I could continue to hold my negative feelings about the traffic snarl and refuse to enjoy the concert. Or, I could release all that messy emotional garbage, take a deep breath and enjoy the beautiful music. I chose to enjoy the concert, and I have a great memory of the experience. The "screech" of the traffic, and the rudeness of the drivers, are still somewhere in my memory banks, but I disconnected them from my emotional enjoyment of the concert.

A day trip to the beach with the family that ends with a flat tire on the way home can present the same dilemma. Do you remember the good memories of the happiness of the family anticipation and planning a trip to the beach and splashing in the waves and eating corndogs on the boardwalk and making sandcastles with the kids while you are at the beach? What about the happy drive home when everyone is tired, sandy, and talking about the great time they had at the beach, until the tire goes flat?

How will you remember the trip to the beach in 30 days?

Dr. Kahneman explained more about this with another example. When visiting the doctor, he will ask, " does it hurt when I pull your arm?" and the remembering self will remember if it hurt or not. The remembering self "keeps score and keeps the history of our life." It remembers the vacations and the fights with our spouse and the good and bad things. Getting confused between the two selves is "part of the mess about the notion of happiness."

The remembering self is a storyteller, and the stories are the only thing we get to keep from our experiences, aside from the souvenirs we purchase or pictures we take. When two of your children go to the doctor to get a shot, each will experience some pain. However, their memory of the pain, how much pain they *think* they had can be vastly different. A younger child may think there was more pain, and an older child may think there was less pain. His memory is much more favorable and different than that of his sibling.

What defines a story are changes, significant moments, and endings, all of which are very important. Our experiencing self is continuously experiencing life moment by moment, and most moments are about three brief seconds long. We lose most of these moments, or we ignore them. They are not recalled by the remembering self. These are two distinct selves and the most significant difference is how they handle *time*.

If you have had two colonoscopies with different doctors or at different facilities, which ever one you remember as the best experience is the one you will choose for your third procedure. The remembering self makes decisions about how good or bad the first two procedures were. We don't choose between experiences, we choose between *memories* of experiences. If the experiences with the doctors were both alright, but the first facility was very cold, you may choose the second facility.

We may also look at the future as anticipated memories rather than anticipated experiences. We consume the memories of our experiences. If you had a very wonderful beach vacation last year, you would remember it more often and enjoy the memory. Was it really better than the beach vacation where you got severely sunburned, exhausted, had sand in your hair, a flat tire, and the kids argued the whole way there?

Truth be told, the kids argued during the entire trip to the beach last year, but you had a new vehicle and were enamored of all the fancy bells and whistles, so you remember the memory of the pleasant drive to the beach in the new car with all the fancy stuff. It was more enjoyable because you had a tire pressure indicator that alerted you to the tire that was losing air. You stopped to fill the tire before it was flat, so you remembered that joyful experience in the new car, namely that you did not have a flat tire on the way home when you were tired and had sand in your hair. You do not remember that the kids argue every year whether they are in an old car or a new car. The trip in the new car seems to be more happy and you remember it as being more happy, because you did not have a flat tire and you had a new car.

After reviewing the *TED talk* several times, I started to unpack some memories and began to grapple with some daunting and negative memories. Over time, as I studied this new information and used it in my own circumstances, my perspective changed. I moved from negative to positive and found a good measure of peace and contentment with rebuilt memories.

It was liberating to make peace with some painful memories and helpful to learn about my remembering self and experiencing self and being happy with my life. I sincerely hope you will find this information useful in your life. To view the *TED talk* by Dr. Kahneman, go here: https://www.ted.com/talks/daniel_kahneman_the_riddle_of_experience_vs_memory

Closing Thoughts

Leading Yourself: A Beneficial, Silly Story About a Coke Bottle

Individuals who lead cannot stand still. They must constantly renew and refresh their thought processes, examine their intentions, and reflect on their actions. We need to be teachable, flexible, and humble—and recognize when we should adjust our perspective. Stories from our friends, neighbors, and communities can play a large role in helping us see where and when we need self-improvement. This is one such story, called "silly" by the author.[1] It is actually wise, illuminating, and quite beneficial.

Pastor-Missionary Craig Ford and his family served in Papua New Guinea for several years. He shared this story about how they were very blessed in 2011, and they decided to share this prosperity with their community. They invited their friends and neighbors to a feast. The family prepared meats and purchased ice cream, chocolate cake and Coke, which are luxury items in the villages where they served. There was enough food for double servings and take-home plates from the Saturday night celebration.

At the end of the party, several people asked for an empty *Coke* bottle to use to take cold water home—even that is a rare treat in some areas. The Pastor filled two bottles with cold water. Then another person asked. He could only locate one more bottle. And he knew that if he gave away that last bottle, he would have no clean water during the church service the next morning.

There are no public water sources where the worship services are held.

He said, "That's when it struck me. All of the food and all of the time preparing was convenient for me to give. Essentially, it wasn't sacrificial because I got to choose what and when to give. I planned the party so that when everything was done, I'd still have all I wanted. But, this *Coke* bottle was something I really wanted to have. Since I preach on Sundays, I often *need* water to keep me hydrated and clear my throat."[2]

Pastor Craig was reluctant to part with the bottle, but God was dealing with his heart. When the family spent hundreds of dollars to feed the community, it was a willing choice. Giving the *Coke* bottle away was a surrender to God's will and an act of sacrificial giving to others. God swiftly honored his decision. The pastor said, "After the party, I drove folks home. When I dropped off the last person, I looked between the seats, and guess what I found … an empty *Coke* bottle. It was like manna from heaven. Perhaps I'm reading too much into this little story, but I think God was reminding me that it's okay to give up precious things because He'll still take care of us."[3]

This "silly" little story has tremendous value, and it is brimming with meaning about the intentional *choice* to give a sacrificial gift. An empty *Coke* bottle is a mundane item. Some would consider to be a piece of trash. But there are some who treasure it.

The story is profound, in that, it dealt with the process of softening the heart, to remove selfishness, replacing it with regard for others. Like it says in Ezekiel 36:26, *"I will give you a new heart and put a new spirit in you; I will remove from you your heart of stone and give you a heart of flesh."*

It illuminated the blessings of sacrificial giving. 1 King 17:13-15, tells the story of Elijah the prophet and the widow and her son. Elijah said to her, *"…first make a small loaf of bread for me from what you have and bring it to me....this is what the Lord, the God of Israel, says: 'The jar of flour will not be used up and the jug of oil will not run dry until the day the Lord sends rain on the land.'"*

It promotes recall of the very words of Christ about giving a cup (or bottle) of cold water to "the least of these." Matthew 10:42, recounts His words, *"And if anyone gives even a cup of cold water to one of these little ones who is my disciple, truly I tell you, that person will certainly not lose their reward."*

Positive Leadership: A Hope Generator

In 2015, Gina Hollenbeck, an avid marathon runner and tennis player, developed a persistent cough, experienced weight loss, and had a host of other health problems. She consulted her physician, and the first diagnosis was seasonal allergies. Then it was acid reflux. Yet a third diagnosis said it was a pulled muscle. She was given medication by each doctor who treated her. When none of the medications worked, she strongly suspected something else was wrong.

Gina sought a chest X-ray, but her doctors and insurance company did not agree. She was a non-smoker. She paid for a chest X-ray on her own. It was $75.00 expense that saved her life. The diagnosis was stage four lung cancer that had metastasized to her brain. When she sought treatment, one oncologist told her she had ten months to live. She did not accept that and then consulted with *Baptist Cancer Center* and Oncology Specialist Dr. Raymond Osarogiagbon.

When she asked the oncologist how long she had and her chances for survival, Dr. Osarogiagbon said, "You know Gina, statistics are statistics, but your story is your own, and I'm gonna do everything I can to cure this disease." He stayed positive, gave her a seed of hope, and then worked hard to make that hope grow from seed, to bloom and remission. He did everything possible, including testing the cancer, adjusting targeted gene therapy, and when hope faded, finding a new therapy only recently authorized by the FDA. Following 37 months of grueling treatment and recurrence, she was declared cancer-free and joyfully and gratefully celebrates her victory each day of her life.[4]

Gina is a great example of self-advocacy and leading herself well. She knew something was wrong and persevered in seeking answers that eventually saved her life. Dr. Osarogiagbon is a hope generator. Proverbs 13:12 says, *"Hope deferred makes the heart sick, but a longing fulfilled is a tree of life."* In that "lollipop moment" he was the one person who positively impacted her life for the best possible outcome.

Mud and Stars: Control Where You Look

"In every situation you have the opportunity to look at the good or look at the bad. There's mud and stars in every opportunity. You can't always control your situation that you're in, but you can control where you look. So for me, it's stars baby, all the way."
—Gina Hollenbeck

Positive leadership involves inspiring positive emotions. Dr. Osarogiagbon took the opportunity to look at the good, the possible, and the positive. He was able to influence the thinking and outlook of his patient. He did not give her a guarantee or a promise he could not keep, but he did not rule out hope.

Leadership consultant T. J. Addington writes on his blog, "Real leaders have influence over others, whether they are in positions of leadership or not. They have a positive influence on others and are a purveyor of hope. Leaders are optimistic about the future and convey that optimism by giving hope to those they lead."[5] They choose to look at the stars instead of the mud.

I hope you do too.

*"I spent part of my life in ignorance,
saying and doing unwise, unkind, hurtful and offensive things.
My desire is to do better and be better each day,
working on progress, striving toward perfection.
I'm spending the remainder of life serving God with excellence,
loving others as I am loved and being grateful and humble.
My life is forever changed, illuminated now by the
Light of the World."*
—Linda D.

Recommended Reading:

Addington, T. J. Deep Influence. Unseen Practices That Will Revolutionize Your Leadership. Colorado Springs: Navpress, 2014.

Bryant, John Hope. Love Leadership: The New Way to Lead in a Fear-Based World. San Francisco: Jossey-Bass, 2009.

Cloud, Henry. Anything by this author.

Collins, James C. Good to Great: Why Some Companies Make the Leap ... and Others Don't. New York: Harper Business, 2001.

Drucker, Peter F. People and Performance. Boston: Harvard Business School Press, 2007.

Greer, Peter and Phil Smith. Created to Flourish. How Employment Based Solutions Help Eradicate Poverty. Lancaster: HOPE, 2016.

Hovind, Chad. Godonomics: How to Save Our Country and Protect Your Wallet Through Biblical Principles of Finance. Colorado Springs: Multnomah Books, 2013.

Kahneman, Daniel. Thinking, Fast And Slow. New York: Farrar, Straus & Giroux, 2011.

Kotter, John P. Leading Change. Boston: Harvard Business Review Press, 2012.

Kouzes, James M., and Barry Z. Posner. Encouraging the Heart. A Leader's Guide to Rewarding and Recognizing Others. San Francisco: Jossey-Bass, 1999.

---------*The Leadership Challenge: How to Make Extraordinary Things Happen in Organizations*. Hoboken: Jossey-Bass 2012.

Maxwell, John C. Anything by this author.

Miller, Mark. The Heart of Leadership. Becoming a Leader People Want to Follow. San Francisco: Berrett-Koehler, 2013.

Thaler, Richard H., and Cass R Sunstein. Nudge: Improving Decisions About Health, Wealth, and Happiness. Rev. and expanded ed. New York: Penguin Books, 2009.

Ziglar, Hilary Hinton (Zig). Anything by this author.

The Economist and Wired Magazine

About the Author

Linda Dougherty has been married to Joe for 28 years and is a life-long resident of sunny Central Florida. She loves Jesus, her family, a great cup of coffee and chickens, having a fondness for the whimsical artistry of Chef Jacques Pepin and other rooster aficionados. On a recent second honeymoon trip with Joe they travelled to southern France and visited castles and cathedrals. She retired after thirty plus years in the insurance industry and has been involved in church ministry and administrative leadership for over 25 years. Linda volunteered and worked at a local rescue mission and has a heart for the at risk and underserved population. She has been a facilitator of Financial Peace University since 2001 and is currently the leader of People's Life Institute. This is a non-denominational Christian ministry organization with the mission to provide spiritual, economic and practical helps to assist clients toward self-sufficiency and stability. Linda has a BS in Economics and recently graduated from Louisiana Baptist University with a PhD from the School of Christian Communications and Leadership.

Reference Notes

PREFACE:

[1] Butt, Howard. H. E. Butt Foundation. ND Accessed 25 Mar 2019. https://hebfdn.org/portfolio/eisenhower-on-leadership/

INTRODUCTION:

[1] NPR. Web. *"Should Juveniles be sent to jail for life?"* 29 Oct 2009. Accessed 23 Mar 2019.

[2] Whitten, Sara. CNBC. Restaurants. "Papa John's missteps and mistakes have Wall Street wondering whether the pizza chain is beyond recovery." 25 Jul 2018. Accessed 14 May 2019.

[3] BrainyQuote. Web. ND. https://www.brainyquote.com/quotes/jane_velezmitchell_641605

[4] Gale, Eric. The Christian Jedi. Web. "The Redemption of Darth Vader and Nebuchadnezzar." ND. Accessed 15 Dec 2019. https://thechristianjedi.com/the-redemption-of-darth-vader-and-nebuchadnezzar/

CHAPTER ONE: WHAT IS A LEADER?

[1] "Benjamin Hooks." AZQuotes.com. Wind and Fly LTD, 2020. 04 March 2020. https://www.azquotes.com/quote/592072

[2] "Peter Drucker." AZQuotes.com. Wind and Fly LTD, 2020. 04 March 2020. https://www.azquotes.com/quote/859605

[3] Posner, Barry Z. TEDxTalks. "Why Credibility is the Foundation of Leadership." 05 Feb 2015. Accessed 24 Jun 2019. https://www.youtube.com/watch?v=QmMcSBQvQLQ

[4] Sun, Carolyn. "5 Life Lessons from Bill Gates." *Entrepreneur Magazine*. 28 Oct 2016. Accessed 10 Oct 2019. https://www.entrepreneur.com/slideshow/275982

[5] *Holocaust Encyclopedia (June 10, 2013). "Southern Europe". Deportations to Killing Centers. United States Holocaust Memorial Museum.* Accessed 29 Aug 2019.

[6] United Way. Blog. https://www.unitedway.org/blog/bill-gates-dedicates-mary-m.-gates-learning-center-at-united-way. 14 Oct 2010. Accessed 12 Oct 2019.

[7] Churchill, Winston. "Diplomacy." *International Churchill Society.* Accessed 24 Jun 2019.

[8] Dixon, Leticia. "Mein Kampf." Encyclopedia Britannica. 04 Jan 2019. https://www.britannica.com/topic/Mein-Kampf Accessed 24 Jun 2019.

[9] Reuters. UN Watch. 12 Nov. 2015 https://www.reuters.com/news/maduro-defends-record-at-un-rights-forum.

[10] Nebehay, Stephanie. UN rights boss sees possible "crimes against humanity" in Venezuela. Reuters. 11 Sept 2017. https://ca.reuters.com/article/topNews/idCAKCN1BM0UI-OCATP. Accessed 24 May 2019.

[11] Hansler, Jennifer. CNN. Web. "US oil executives moved from house arrest to prison after Guaido meets with Trump." 07 Feb 2020.

[12] Williams, Walter. Speech given at Foundation of Economic Education Annual Forum. 28 Jun 2014. https://fee.org/articles/walter-williams-at-fee/ Accessed 22 Jul 2019.

[13] Sowell, Thomas. "Farewell to Economist and Teacher Walter E. Williams, My Best Friend." *Daily Signal.* 03 Dec 2020. Accessed 05 Jan 2021. https://www.dailysignal.com/2020/12/03/farewell-to-economist-and-teacher-walter-e-williams-my-best-friend/?utm_source=rss&utm_medium=rss&utm_campaign=farewell-to-economist-and-teacher-walter-e-williams-my-best-friend

[14] Neuharth-Keusch, A.J. "Dolphins Sign Mark Walton." USA TODAY. 12 May 2019 https://www.usatoday.com/story/sports/nfl/2019/05/12/mark-walton-dolphins/1183642001/ Accessed 24 Jun 2019.

[15] ESPN. Web. NFL. *"Ex-Dolphins RB Mark Walton faces 2nd domestic assault accusation."* 03 Jan 2020. Accessed 14 Jan 2020. https://www.espn.com/nfl/story/_/id/28415168/ex-dolphins-rb-mark-walton-faces-2nd-domestic-assault-accusation.

[16] Piazza, Jo. "How much can a Celebrity make for Tweeting?" *Vulture. The Celebrity Economy. New York Magazine.* 28 Jan 2012. https://www.vulture.com/2012/01/how-much-can-a-celebrity-make-for-tweeting.html Accessed 21 Jun 2019.

[17] Jones, Stacy. "How Much Kim Kardashian Charges for An Instagram Post" Blog. *Hollywood Branded.* 27 Nov 2017. https://blog.hollywoodbranded.com/how-much-kim-kardashian-charges-for-an-instagram-post. Accessed 21 Jun 2019.

[18] Taylor, Kate. "How Much Kim Kardashian charges for Instagram endorsement." *Business Insider.* 5 May 2019. https://www.businessinsider.com/how-much-kim-kardashian-charges-for-instagram-endorsement-deals-2019-5. Accessed 21 Jun 2019.

[19] Frey, Kaitlyn. "This Is the Most Real Photo Kim Kardashian Has Ever Shared of Her Psoriasis." Style. *People Magazine.* 01 Jul 2019. Accessed 10 Sep 2019. https://people.com/style/kim-kardashian-shares-psoriasis-struggle-photo/

[20] Ramsey, Dave. @DaveRamsey. 2:00PM 24 Jul 2018. Accessed 14 Feb 2020.

CHAPTER TWO: WHAT IS LEADERSHIP?

[1] *"Dwight D Eisenhower Quotes." Quotes.net.* STANDS4 LLC, 2020. Web. 3 Mar. 2020. <https://www.quotes.net/quote/246>.

[2] Warren Bennis Quotes. BrainyQuote. Web. 3 Mar 2020. https://www.brainyquote.com/quotes/warren_bennis_121713

[3] "-ship". *Dictionary.com* Dictionary.com LLC. Accessed 26 Apr 2019.

[4] Baldoni, John. "Putting the Art of Leadership into Practice." Leadership Development. *Harvard Business Review.* 18 Sep 2009. Accessed 14 Sep 2019. https://hbr.org/2009/09/putting-the-art-of-leadership

[5] Bastianich, Lidia. HelloCheffy.

[6] Drucker, Peter F. *The Practice of Management.* Oxford. Elsevier Ltd. 1955. Page 138.

[7] Maxwell, John C. *My Purpose.* https://www.johnmaxwell.com/my-purpose/ Accessed 12 Apr 2019.

[8] Paraphrase from ideas in: J.M. Kouzes and B.Z. Posner, "Credibility: How Leaders Gain and Lose It, Why People Demand It" (San Francisco, California: Jossey-Bass, 2011)

[9] "Colin Powell." AZQuotes.com. Wind and Fly LTD, 2020. 04 March 2020. https://www.azquotes.com/quote/235164

[10] Esheninger, Eric. "Great Leaders Surround Themselves with Smart People.". *A Principal's Reflections.* http://esheninger.blogspot.com/2018/07/great-leaders-surround-themselves-with.html 19 Jul 2018. Accessed 14 May 2019.

[11] Hyatt, Michael. "Why Leaders Exist." Leadership. MichaelHyatt.com. 29 Nov 2010. Accessed 28 Aug 2019. https://michaelhyatt.com/why-leaders-exist/

[12] Gonzalez, Gabriel. Ospina-Valencia, José, Deutsche Welle. Americas. "Venezuela's opposition sees a trap in Maduro's preelection pardons" 02 Sep 20. Accessed 01 Oct 2020. https://www.dw.com/en/venezuelas-opposition-sees-a-trap-in-maduros-preelection-pardons/a-54796068

[13] Saliba, Emmanuelle, Euronews, Gutierrez,. "Video shows strangers rescue baby from watery grave in Texas." NBC News. 01 May 2017. Accessed 21 Jun 2019. https://www.nbcnews.com/news/us-news/video-shows-strangers-rescue-infants-watery-grave-texas-n753436

[14] Purdy, Lucy. Item #18. *Positive News.* Society/World. 28 Jun 2019. Accessed 28 Jun 2019. https://www.positive.news/society/what-went-right-january-june-2019/.

[15] "What We Do: Malaria Strategy Overview." *Bill and Melinda Gates Foundation.* Accessed 24 Jun 2019. https://www.gatesfoundation.org/What-We-Do/Global-Health/Malaria.

CHAPTER THREE: WHAT SHOULD IT LOOK LIKE?

[1] Brinson, Jay. *Influence People Like Jesus.* Springfield. 21st Century Press. 2017. Page 85.

[2] Elmore, Tim. "Is Everyone A Leader?" Artificial Maturity. *Psychology Today.* 20 Feb 2014. Accessed 22 May 2019.
https://www.psychologytoday.com/us/blog/artificial-maturity/201402/is-everyone-leader

[3] Elmore, Tim. @Tim Elmore. 10:45 AM · 14 Feb 2020. Accessed 14 Feb 2020.

[4] Dudley, Drew. "Leading with Lollipops." TEDxToronto. 07 Oct 2010. Accessed 17 May 2019.
https://www.youtube.com/watch?v=hVCBrkrFrBE

[5] Ibid.

[6] Ibid.

[7] Ibid.

[8] Internet Archive. Wayback Machine. Profile on Dr. Muhammad Yunus. 10 Oct 2006. Accessed 10 Sep 2019.
https://web.archive.org/web/20061017160138/http://www.bangladeshnews.com.bd/2006/10/14/profile-dr-muhammad-yunus/

[9] Ibid.

CHAPTER FOUR: ARE LEADERS MADE OR BORN?

[1] Bromley, Melanie. ENews. Web. "The Reinvention of Prince Harry: How Those Naked Vegas Pictures Helped Turn His Life Around" 22 Aug 2016. Accessed 14 Jun 2019.

https://www.eonline.com/news/789026/the-reinvention-of-prince-harry-how-those-naked-vegas-pictures-helped-turn-his-life-around

[2] Posner, Barry Z. "From Inside Out: Beyond Teaching About Leadership." *Journal of Leadership Education*. 10 Mar 2009. Page 2. https://law.scu.edu/wp-content/uploads/leadership/Journal%20of%20Leadership%20Education%20March%202009(1).pdf Accessed 13 Jun 2019.

[3] Ibid.

[4] Elmore, Tim. Psychology Today. Web. "Is Everyone a Leader?" 14 Feb 2014. Accessed 20 Mar 2019.

https://www.psychologytoday.com/za/blog/artificial-maturity/201402/is-everyone-leader?amp

[5] Ibid.

[6] *Hersey, P. & Blanchard, K. H. "Life cycle theory of leadership". Training and Development Journal. 1969. Vol. 23. Issue 5. Print. Pages 26–34.*

[7] Savage, Mark. "Ringo Starr receives Knighthood." *BBC. Arts and Entertainment.* 20 Mar 2018. https://www.bbc.com/news/entertainment-arts-43472196. Accessed 24 Jun 2019.

[8] *Micallef, Ken; Marshall, Donnie. Classic Rock Drummers. Backbeat Books. 2007. p. 95.*

[9] *Flans, Robyn. "Ringo Starr" PAS Hall of Fame. Percussive Arts Society.* https://www.pas.org/about/hall-of-fame/ringo-starr. *Accessed 15 Jun 2019.*

[10] Browning, Peter. Sparks, William. "Are Leaders made or born—or both?" *Charlotte Business Journal.* 27 Sep 2002. Accessed 15 Jun 2019. http://drwillsparks.com/wp-content/uploads/2011/03/CBJ-Are-Leaders-Born-or-Made.pdf

[11] Carlyle T. *On Heroes, Hero-worship, and the Heroic in History.* Project Gutenberg; 2012. http://www.gutenberg.org/files/1091/1091-h/1091-h.htm. Accessed 28 Apr 2019.

[12] "Intrinsic." *Merriam-Webster.com Dictionary*, Merriam-Webster, https://www.merriam-webster.com/dictionary/intrinsic. Accessed 28 Apr 2019.

[13] Spencer, Herbert. *The Study of Sociology*, Appleton, 1896, pp. 30- 31. https://www.questia.com/read /96277798/the-study-of-sociology

[14] Boerma, Marjan et al. "Point/Counterpoint: Are Outstanding Leaders Born or Made?" *American Journal Of Pharmaceutical Education* vol. 81,3 (2017): 58. doi:10.5688/ajpe81358. Accessed 28 Apr 2019.

[15] Ashkenas, Ron. Hausmann, Robert. "Leadership Development should focus on Experiments." *Harvard Business Review.* 12 Apr 2016. Accessed 24 Jun 2019. *https://hbr.org/2016/04/leadership-development-should-focus-on-experiments*

CHAPTER FIVE: KNOWING AND LEADING YOURSELF

[1] *The Empire Strikes Back.* Dir. George W. Lucas. Perf. Frank Oz. 20th Century Fox. 1977. Film.

[2] *Return of the Jedi.* Dir. Richard Marquand. Perf. Frank Oz. 20th Century Fox. 1983. Film.

[3] Ziglar OnDemand. Show #346: You must see more in yourself." ND. 26 Jan 2019. https://www.ziglar.com/show/seemoreinyou/

[4] Addington, T. J. "Why defensiveness is destructive and how we can become more open." *Leading from the Sandbox.* 20 Dec. 2018. Web. Accessed 22 Jan. 2019. https://leadingfromthesandbox.blogspot.com 2018/12/why-defensiveness-is-destructive-to-and.html

[5] Ibid. "Managing anxiety in our leadership roles and saving us from ourselves." 09 May 2015. Accessed 24 Jan 2019. Managing anxiety in our leadership roles and saving us from ourselves

[6] Drucker, Peter F. Harvard Business Review. Cambridge. Best of HBR 1999. "Managing Oneself" Pg. 100.

[7] "Self-Awareness Theory." International Encyclopedia of the Social Sciences. . *Encyclopedia.com.* 20 Jan. 2019 <https://www.encyclopedia.com>.

[8] Addington, T. J. *Deep Influence.* Colorado Springs. NavPress. 2014. Page 187.

[9] Obama, Michelle. CNN. Speech. Broadcast. 25 Jul 2016. 20 Jan 2019. https://www.youtube.com/ watch?v =mu_hCThhzWU

[10] Gollwitzer, Peter. Fortune. Tools of the Trade. "How to Break Bad Habits Once and for All." 26 Jan 2017. Web. Accessed 20 Jan 2019. http://fortune.com/2017/01/25/how-to-break-bad-habits-2/

CHAPTER SIX: LEADERSHIP CREDIBILITY

[1] News Release. UC Davis Press Release. "Tiger Woods Scandal Cost Shareholders up to $12 Billion" 04 Dec 2009. Accessed 15 Jul 2019. http://gsm.ucdavis.edu/news-release/tiger-woods-scandal-cost-shareholders-12-billion

[2] Rolex: Every Rolex tells a Story: Tiger Woods. Web. 2019. https://www.rolex.com/every-rolex-tells-a-story/tiger-woods-rolex-watch.html. Accessed 22 Sep 2019.

[3] Maddeus, Gene. Variety. *"CBS Credit Union Manager Sentenced for Fraud."16* Sep 2019. Accessed 28 Sep 2019. https://variety.com/2019/biz/news/cbs-credit-union-manager-sentenced-fraud-1203337640/

[4] Ibid.

[5] United States Department of Justice. Central District of California. Press Release. 16 Sep 2019. Accessed 28 Sep 2019.
https://www.justice.gov/usao-cdca/pr/ex-credit-union-manager-sentenced-more-14-years-federal-prison-40-million-embezzlement

CHAPTER SEVEN: WHAT IS FAILURE?

[1] Pallardy, Richard. Deepwater Horizon Oil Spill. Encyclopedia Britannica. Web. ND. Accessed Oct. 2, 2019.
https://www.britannica.com/event/Deepwater-Horizon-oil-spill/Environmental-costs

[2] Broder, John M. New York Times. *"Panel Says Firms Knew of Cement Flaws Before Spill."* 28 Oct 2010. Accessed 28 Sep 2019.
https://www.nytimes.com/2010/10/29/us/29spill.html

[3] Kouzes, James. Posner, Barry. "We Lead from the Inside Out." *The Journal of Values-Based Leadership.* Vol. 1; Issue 1. Winter 2008. Page 2.
https://scholar.valpo.edu/cgi/viewcontent.cgi?article=1004&context=jvb
l Business Commons. Accessed 12 Oct 2019.

[4] *Moseley, G. Lorimer; Parsons, Timothy J.; Spence, Charles (2008). "Visual distortion of a limb modulates the pain and swelling evoked by movement". Current Biology. **18** (22): R1047–R1048. doi:10.1016/j.cub.2008.09.031.*

[5] Emmons, Robert. Greater Good Magazine. Mind and Body. *"Why Gratitude is Good."* 16 Nov 2010. Accessed 12 Nov 2019.
https://greatergood.berkeley.edu/article/item/why_gratitude_is_good

[6] Cuban, Mark. BlogMaverick. *"The best equity is sweat equity."* 02 Jan 2008. Accessed 12 Nov 2019.

[1] Proverbs 30:8 (need translation)

CHAPTER EIGHT: WHAT IS SUCCESS?

[2] *Fonda, Daren. Time. "Motor Trends: Le Cost Killer". 19 May 2003. Accessed 30 Oct 2019.*

[3] Chozick, Amy and Rich, Motoko. The New York Times. *"The Rise and Fall of Carlos Ghosn."* 30 Dec 2018. Section A. Pg 1. Accessed 28 Oct 2019

[4] Martin Winterkorn. Forbes. Lists. Powerful People 2014. ND. Accessed 26 Oct 2019. https://www.forbes.com/profile/martin-winterkorn/#296c2ca0432a

[5] Kottasova, Irana. CNN Business. "German prosecutors charge former Volkswagen CEO Martin Winterkorn with fraud." 15 Apr 2019. Accessed 25 Oct 2019. https://www.cnn.com/2019/04/15/business/winterkorn-volkswagen-diesel-fraud-charges/index.html

[6] Coppella, Leah. The Charlatan. Web. *"Drew Dudley on Success and Leadership."* 10 Sep 2017. Accessed 27 Oct 2019. https://charlatan.ca/2017/09/qa-drew-dudley-on-success-and-leadership/

[7] Rascanu, Alex. Web Blog. "How to Reach your Potential: An interview with Drew Dudley." 03 Oct 2017. Accessed 27 Oct 2019. https://www.rascanu.com/blog/drew-dudley

[8] Dudley, Drew. "The Leadership Game: Creating cultures of Leadership." TEDxAnchorage. 09 Oct 2014. Accessed 12 Oct 2019. https://www.youtube.com/watch?v=EuB9S6fzMig

[9] Ibid.

[10] Ibid.

[11] Schawbel, Dan. Forbes. Web. *"Zig Ziglar's Tips for becoming successful in life."* 11 Aug 2011. Accessed 27 Oct 2019.

https://www.forbes.com/sites/danschawbel/2011/08/11/zig-ziglars-tips-on-becoming-successful-in-life/#6b5a584d6d89

[12] Ibid.

[13] Ibid.

[14] Wooden, John. "True Success." TEDed. Monterey. Published 24 Aug 2013. Accessed 27 Oct 2019.
https://www.youtube.com/watch?v=3s_hlvhwmvg

[15] Breakfast with Fred. Success Articles. Weekly Thought. "Permitting Success." 10 Sep 2019. Accessed 15 Jan 2019.
https://www.bwfli.com/category/weekly-thoughts/success/

[16] Ibid.

CHAPTER NINE: ORGANIZATIONAL FAILURE AND RECOVERY

[1] Mullaney, Tim. CNBC. "The CEO Warren Buffett turn to for Wisdom" 5 April 2017. Accessed: June 12, 2018.
https://www.cnbc.com/2017/03/08/the-ceo-warren-buffett-turns-to-for-wisdom-jpmorgans-jamie-dimon.html

[2] Buffett, Warren. Berkshire Hathaway. *Annual Shareholder Letter*. Page 7. 23 Feb 2019. Accessed 12 Jul 2019.
https://www.berkshirehathaway.com/letters/2018ltr.pdf

[3] Cheng, Evelyn. Crippen, Alex. CNBC. Investing. "Warren Buffett: I was wrong on Google and 'too dumb' to appreciate Amazon." 08 May 2017. Accessed 27 Aug 2019.
https://www.cnbc.com/2017/05/06/warren-buffett-admits-he-made-a-mistake-on-google.html

[4] Williams, Sean. "Warren Buffett's Biggest Blunder has now cost him $16 Billion." Motley Fool. Investing. Web.

27 Aug 2019. Accessed 22 Oct 2019. https://www.fool.com/investing/2019/08/27/warren-buffetts-biggest-blunder-has-now-cost-him-1.aspx

[5] Horwood, Clive. Lee, Peter. Euromoney. *"The bankers that define the decades: Jamie Dimon, JPMorgan Chase."* 10 June 2019. Accessed 29 Oct 2019. https://www.euromoney.com/article/b1fq6yftgm9nrv/the-bankers-that-define-the-decades-jamie-dimon-jpmorgan-chase?copyrightInfo=true

[6] Dimon, Jamie. "What Makes a Good Leader?" Chase. Leadership. Web. Updated 10 Nov 2017. Accessed 17 Mar 2018. https://www.chase.com/news/111614-jamie-dimon-hallmarks-of-a-good-leader

[7] JP Morgan Case and Co. Website. About Us. Awards and Recognition. Accessed 27 Oct 2019. https://www.jpmorganchase.com/corporate/About-JPMC/ab-awards.htm

[8] Dimon, Jamie. "What Makes a Good Leader?" Chase. Leadership. Web. Updated 10 Nov 2017. Accessed 17 Mar 2018. https://www.chase.com/news/111614-jamie-dimon-hallmarks-of-a-good-leader

[8] JP Morgan Case and Co. Website. About Us. Awards and Recognition. Accessed 27 Oct 2019.

[9] Trugman, Jonathon. NY Post. "JP Morgan is Thriving under Dimon a decade after Financial crisis." 21 July 2018. Accessed 27 July 2018. https://nypost.com/2018/07/21/jpmorgan-is-thriving-under-dimon-a-decade-after-financial-crisis/

[10] Smoak, Anthony. Web. "The London Whale Trading Incident." 27 Dec 2018. Accessed 22 Jun 2019. https://anthonysmoak.com/2018/12/27/the-london-whale-trading-incident/

[11] Schaefer, Steve. Forbes. Markets. "Jamie Dimon: What I learned from the London Whale." 10 April 2013. Accessed 12 Jun 2018. https://www.forbes.com/sites/steveschaefer/2013/04/10/jamie-dimon-what-i-learned-from-the-london-whale/#4669c8f6797

[12] Smoak, Anthony. Web. "The London Whale Trading Incident." 27 Dec 2018. Accessed 22 Jun 2019. https://anthonysmoak.com/2018/12/27/the-london-whale-trading-incident/

[13] J.P. Morgan Chase. *2014 Annual Report, Jamie Dimon's Letter*. 2014. Web. 20 April 2015.

[14] McDonald, Duff. New York Magazine. "How Jamie Dimon put himself in the position for deal of the century." 21 Mar 2008. Accessed 22 Jun 2019. https://nymag.com/news/features/45320/

[15] Ibid.

[16] Fernandez, Henry. FoxBusiness. Web. "JP Morgan Chase CEO Jamie Dimon Taps Two Women Execs as potential successors." 18 Apr 2019. Accessed 27 Jun 2019. https://www.foxbusiness.com/business-leaders/jpmorgan-chase-ceo-jamie-dimon-women-execs-successors

[17] Aboulafia, Richard. Forbes. *"Boeing, McNerney and the high price of treating aircraft like it was any other industry."* 24 Jun 2015. Accessed 22 Jul 2019. https://www.forbes.com/sites/richardaboulafia/2015/06/24/boeing-mcnerney-and-the-high-price-of-treating-aircraft-like-it-was-any-other-industry/#1e6baa3b579c

[18] Ibid.

[19] Ibid.

[20] Mutzabugh, Ben. USA Today. Web. "Happy birthday, 737! Boeing's workhorse turns 50." 10 Apr 2017. Accessed 7 Jul 2019. https://www.usatoday.com/story/travel/flights/todayinthesky/2017/04/10/celebration-boeing-737-50-years-flying/100282086/

[21] Gelles, Karl, Loehrke, Janet, Padilla, Ramon. Petras, George. USA TODAY. "What's Next for the 737 MAX—and Boeing?" 06 Feb 2020. Accessed 18 Feb 2020.

[22] Josephs, Leslie. CNBC. "Southwest Airlines Profits Tumble…" 23 Jan 2020. Accessed 28 Jan 2020.
https://www.cnbc.com/2020/01/23/southwest-luv-earnings-q4-beat-estimates.html

[23] Gelles, Karl, Loehrke, Janet, Padilla, Ramon. Petras, George. USA TODAY. "What's Next for the 737 MAX—and Boeing?" 06 Feb 2020. Accessed 18 Feb 2020.

[24] Beech, Hannah. Suhartono, Muktita. "In Boeing Lion Air Crash, Indonesians Learn what took their Loved Ones." The New York Times. 23 Oct 2019. Accessed 14 Nov 2019.

[25] Ibid.

[26] Ladd, Brittan. The Observer. "Why the 737 Max should be permanently grounded." 17 May 2019. Accessed 17 Jul 2019.
https://observer.com/2019/05/boeing-737-software-fix-permanently-ground/

[27] Ibid.

[28] Ladd, Brittian. The Observer. "The time has come for the CEO of Boeing to resign." 03 Jun 2019. Accessed 17 Jul 2019.
https://observer.com/2019/06/boeing-ceo-dennis-muilenburg-737-max-crash/

[29] Muilenburg, Dennis. BloomburgTV. Interviewed by Guy Johnson. Web. "Boeing CEO expects 737 MAX to return to service this year." 17 Jun 2019. Accessed 16 Jul 2019.
https://www.bloomberg.com/news/articles/2019-06-16/for-stricken-boeing-paris-air-show-is-about-more-than-jet-sales

[30] Ibid.

[31] Florian, Ellen. Fortune. "Governance Experts on Boeing: There is something wrong with the board." 23 May 2019. Accessed 15 Jul 2019. https://fortune.com/2019/05/23/boeing-board-governance-experts/

[32] Ibid.

[33] Shepardson, David. Reuters. Business News. *"Senior US lawmaker says Boeing must shake up management after 737 Max crashes."* 18 Oct 2019. Accessed 12 Jan 2020. https://www.reuters.com/article/us-ethiopia-airline-congress/senior-u-s-lawmaker-says-boeing-must-shake-up-management-after-737-max-crashes-idUSKBN1WX2HB

[34] Ibid.

[35] Luc, Olinga. Yahoo News. *"Boeing employees' emails bemoan culture of 'arrogance'"* 12 Jan 2020. Accessed 15 Jan 2020. https://www.yahoo.com/news/boeing-employees-emails-bemoan-culture-arrogance-012850407.html

[36] Wallace, Danielle. Fox News. Airlines. *"Boeing employees' emails mocked 737 Max's safety."* 10 Jan 2020. Accessed 15 Jan 2020. https://www.foxnews.com/us/boeing-employees-mock-faa-clowns-monkeys-737-max.

[37] WTTW. Crain's Headlines. Business. *"Potential Safety Hazard Another Embarrassment for Boeing."* 19 Feb 2020. Accessed 22 Feb 2020. https://news.wttw.com/2020/02/19/crain-s-headlines-potential-safety-hazard-another-embarrassment-boeing

[38] Rahadiana, Rieka. Listiyorini, Eko. Levin, Alan. Bloomberg. *"Indonesian Divers Retrieve Flight Recorder from Jet Crash."* 12 Jan 2021. Accessed 13 Jan 2021. https://www.msn.com/en-us/news/world/boeing-officials-get-covid-pass-to-fly-to-indonesia-crash-site/ar-BB1cFeqU

[39] "Ford Pinto Fuel Fed Fires." Web. The Center for Auto Safety. ND. Accessed 10 Oct 2019. https://www.autosafety.org/ford-pinto-fuel-fed-fires/

[40] *Schwartz, Gary T. (1991). "The Myth of the Ford Pinto Case"* (PDF). *Rutgers Law Review.* **43***: 1013–1068.Accessed Oct 17, 2019.*

CHAPTER TEN: PERSONAL FAILURE AND RECOVERY

[1] "System." *The Merriam-Webster.com Dictionary*, Merriam-Webster Inc., https://www.merriam-webster.com/dictionary/system. Accessed 13 Dec 2019.

[2] Henning, Pamela. Wilmshurst, Jacqui. Yearworth, Mike. Journals ISSS. "Understanding Systems Thinking: An Agenda for Applied Research in Industry." 15 Jul 2012 Presentation. Accessed 13 Dec 2019. http://journals.isss.org/index.php/proceedings56th/article/download/1909/612

[3] The Bowen Center for the Study of the Family. Web. Preface. Accessed 27 Oct 2019. http://thebowencenter.org/theory/

[4] Ibid.

[5] Ibid.

[6] Star Trek - First Contact (1996) Archived September 29, 2013, at the Wayback Machine Moviesoundclips.net. Rikeromega3 Productions 1999-2013. Accessed 28 Oct 2019.

[7] Ibid.

[8] The Bowen Center for the Study of the Family. Web. Preface. Accessed 27 Oct 2019. http://thebowencenter.org/theory/

[9] Kerr, Michael, and Murray Bowen. *Family Evaluation: An Approach Based on Bowen Theory.* New York, NY: Norton, 1988. Print. Page 113.

[10] Grant, Adam. (@AdamMGrant.) 5:47 AM - 2 Dec 2019. Tweet.

[11] The Family Systems Institute. Definitions from Bowen's Theory. Differentiation. Accessed 22 Oct 2019. http://www.thefsi.com.au/definitions-bowen-theory/

[12] Brown, Jenny. MacKay, Linda. Australian and New Zealand Journal of Family Therapy. Vol. 34. 2014. Accessed Nov 27 2019. http://www.thefsi.com.au/wp-content/uploads/2013/12/Supervision-Paper-JB-LMK-2014-ANZJFT.pdf

[13] Friedman, Edwin. *Generation to Generation: Family Process in Church and Synagogue* (New York: Guilford Press, 1985), 33-34

[14] Friedman, Edwin. "Bowen Theory and Therapy." *Handbook of Family Therapy*. Edited by Alan S. Gurman and David Kniskern. Vol. II. New York. Routledge. 1991. Print. Pages 140-144.

[15] Creech, R. Robert. "Jesus and Differentiation of Self in the New Testament Gospels." Academia.com. Web. 04 Jul 2008. Accessed 19 Nov 2019. https://www.academia.edu/10205885/Jesus_and_Differentiation_of_Self_in_the_New_Testament_Gospels

[16] Kerr, Michael, and Murray Bowen. *Family Evaluation: An Approach Based on Bowen Theory*. New York, NY: Norton, 1988. Print. Pages 376-377.

[17] "Esprit de corps." *Merriam-Webster.com Dictionary*, Merriam-Webster, https://www.merriam-webster.com/dictionary/esprit%20de%20corps. Accessed 17 Jan 2020.

[18] Brown, Brene. "Listening to Shame." TED2012. Long Beach, CA. Accessed 13 Nov 2019. https://www.ted.com/talks/brene_brown_listening_to_shame/transcript?language=en#t-11705

[19] Okura, Lynn. HuffPost. Web. Brené Brown On Shame: 'It Cannot Survive Empathy' 26 Aug 2013. Accessed Nov 14, 2019. https://www.huffpost.com/entry/brene-brown-shame_n_3807115

CHAPTER ELEVEN: SELF DISCOVERY IS PAINFUL

[1] Daman, Glenn C. "Dealing with Conflict in the Smaller Church," www.ag.org/enrichmentjournal (2005), accessed 22 Dec 2019.

CHAPTER TWELVE: LOSS AND RECOVERY

[1] American Psychological Association, (2006). Forgiveness: A Sampling of Research Results. Washington, DC: Office of International Affairs. Reprinted, 2008. Page 5. Accessed 14 Dec 2019. https://web.archive.org/web/20110626153005/http://www.apa.org/international/resources/forgiveness.pdf

[2] John Hopkins Medicine. Health. "Forgiveness: Your health depends on it." ND. Accessed 27 Oct 2019. https://www.hopkinsmedicine.org/health/wellness-and-prevention/forgiveness-your-health-depends-on-it

[3] Meek, Katheryn Rhoads and McMinn, Mark R., "Forgiveness: More than a Therapeutic Technique" 1997. *Faculty Publications, Grad School of Clinical Psychology.* 144.

[4] American Psychological Association. Transcript. Web. "Interview with Mark R. McMinn about Spiritually Oriented Interventions for Counseling and Psychotherapy." 2011. Accessed 26 Oct 2019. https://www.apa.org/pubs/books/interviews/4317258-mcminn

[5] Frise, Nathan R.; Mcminn, Mark R. "Forgiveness and reconciliation: the differing perspectives of psychologists and Christian theologians." *The Free Library* 22 June 2010. 17 January 2020 <https://www.thefreelibrary.com/Forgiveness and reconciliation: the differing perspectives of...-a0231530217>.

[6] Ibid.

[7] Evans, Tony. Forgiveness. Facebook. 04 Feb 2014. 10:32 AM. Accessed 23 Dec 2019.

CHAPTER TWELVE: LEADING WITH INTEGRITY

[1] Maxwell, John C. Web. Blog. "How to lead when your boss can't (or won't) 01 Oct 2019. Accessed 10 Feb 2020. https://www.johnmaxwell.com/blog/how-to-lead-when-your-boss-cant-or-wont/
[2] Crowley, Michael. Haberman, Maggie. The New York Times. Politics. "Pence Makes Clear There Is No Daylight Between Him and Trump." 03 Oct 2019. Accessed 10 Feb 2020.
[3] Clay Bentley. Facebook. 11 Mar 2020. 5:07pm.
https://www.facebook.com/clay.bentley.1/posts/10157570807143248
[4] Beavers, Olivia. The Hill. "Pence: Leaders should be humble, exercise self-control." 12 Jul 2017. Accessed 10 Feb 2020.

CLOSING THOUGHTS:

[1] Ford, Craig. Money Help For Christians. "A Silly Story about a Coke bottle." 24 Jan 2012. Accessed 14 Aug 2018. moneyhelpforchristians.com/silly-coke-story/
[2] Ibid.
[3] Ibid.
[4] Brody, Barbara. Health. "These 3 Women Were Each Diagnosed With Advanced Lung Cancer—Even Though They Never Smoked." 19 Dec 2019. Accessed Feb 12, 2020. https://www.health.com/condition/lung-cancer/3-nonsmoking-women-diagnosed-with-lung-cancer

[5] Addington, T. J. "The Profile of an Effective Church Leader." Leading from the Sandbox. 01 Jun 2008. Accessed 13 May 2019. https://leadingfromthesandbox.blogspot.com/

www.ingramcontent.com/pod-product-compliance
Lightning Source LLC
Chambersburg PA
CBHW070554100426
42744CB00006B/269